Killing Cousins

Killing Cousins

Murder By Increments Book 2

O.J. Modjeska

About the Author

OJ Modjeska is a historian, criminologist, and author. She graduated from the University of Sydney with a PhD in Modern American History in 2004, and received her Graduate Diploma in Criminology from Sydney Law School in 2015. In 2015 she was awarded the JH McClemens Memorial Prize by Sydney Law School for her scholarship in criminology. Before pursuing a writing career she worked for many years as a legal writer and editor. OJ writes books of narrative non-fiction true crime and disaster analysis. Her debut, "Gone: Catastrophe in Paradise", about the Tenerife air disaster, is an ebook bestseller. "A City Owned" and "Killing Cousins" make up the two-part true crime series "Murder by Increments", now available at all good ebook retailers. If you enjoy this book and would like to receive news of new releases, consider subscribing to OJ's mailing list at the link below.

http://ojmodjeska.blogspot.com.au
www.estoire.co

Publication Details

First published in 2018 by Estoire

Text © OJ Modjeska (Obelia Modjeska), 2018

PART ONE:
BITTER SOIL

Chapter 1

It's squaresville, Ken would say of his hometown, Rochester. There was nothing there; nothing waiting for him but a job at Kodak.

He invoked Kodak often as a convenient shorthand for all the reasons Rochester was a nothing place, hardly fit for a man like him, a man with dreams and ambitions.

The company that actually invented the digital camera in 1975 haplessly dropped it from their line out of fear it would threaten their core business, a decision that ultimately stripped it of its position as the foremost manufacturer of photographic equipment. Kodak became a poster child for postindustrial irrelevance, as did many mid-size cities in the northeast. Ken couldn't see into the future, but he knew Kodak was a place for losers, and so was Rochester.

The other thing Ken always talked about was the cold. Over one hundred inches of snow a year, nine months of which were spent indoors. The townsfolk awoke in darkness at six o'clock and didn't know if it was morning or night. The May Lilac Festival suffered a regular deficiency of lilacs.

The Buonos weren't bothered about the cold and gloom. They had been toughened by endless days working in the hot sun of San Buono, in the Abruzzio region of Italy. In 1919, when Kenneth's mother Frances was born, Rochester was an industrial boomtown. Her parents were among the millions that migrated from Southern and Eastern Europe after the war. They settled in Utica, Syracuse, Buffalo and Rochester in great numbers, and the cities prospered with the influx of labor. The work was hard, the cold and snow horrendous, but there was a good living to be made, new homes, and space to raise families. And that was all that really mattered.

The Buonos were a typical Italian family of their time and place. Devout Catholics, they believed a large family was proof of God's bounty. Frances was one of eight children. Her father worked long, exhausting hours as a manual laborer supporting his expanding brood. Mother was occupied all day with the tasks of managing the household and feeding the children. They were provided for materially, but had little in the way of undivided attention or nurturance from their parents—although such was hardly unusual in Italian migrant families at the time.

Even so, there was perhaps always in Frances a feeling of being overlooked; a hunger for love and attention that seemed forever beyond her grasp. The shy, sweet temperament of Nicholas Bianchi therefore suited her. This was no man about town who she must share with everyone else.

The two met at Jefferson High, where they became fast sweethearts. Even then they were a study in contrasts. Frances was opinionated and liked to take charge. Nicholas was retiring and gentle. He was, according to the mores of the time, an abject failure as a man. He tried to enlist in the army but was rejected because of his phobias of insects and worms, and a chronic stutter, for which he had been mercilessly teased throughout school. He joined the American Brake Shoe company as a laborer, where he would routinely put in twelve-hour days. If he couldn't represent his country he could still do the backbreaking work required of a man with little prospects to put bread on his table, feed a family, and earn some kind of respect in the world. Nobody disputed Nicholas' ability to work, but over time, he developed a gambling habit, and all the punishing hours of labor were often for nothing.

Frances and Nicholas married in 1941, and despite their incompatible natures, in the early years at least, they were thought to be very much in love.

From the beginning Frances knew that she, too, wanted a big family. As soon as they were married, Frances and Nicholas began trying for a baby. Soon, however, it became obvious something was wrong: nothing was happening. She consulted a doctor and learned that not only was she unable to conceive, but that she was suffering a life-threatening condition and needed an immediate hysterectomy.

The procedure was a success, but afterwards, Frances spiraled deep into depression. Her whole life had prepared her for motherhood. The traditional Catholic view held that the birth and rearing of children was a woman's primary purpose. She took her barrenness as a personal failing. The hysterectomy also resulted in premature menopause, further derailing an already perilous emotional state.

Nicholas hated to see his wife so miserable, so it was not difficult for her to persuade him that they should seek an adoption.

The little boy they eventually settled on was the biological son of a young man who shared the same Italian Catholic heritage. Handsome, with fair skin, dark hair, and bright blue eyes, he was just over six pounds at birth and physically robust.

It isn't clear how much the Bianchis knew about his time on earth before he reached their care, but when Frances laid eyes on him, she knew he was the one she wanted. He was perfect.

* * *

Ken's biological mother, Florence King, was a beautiful but dissolute go-go dancer.

Still a teenager, she had already been in and out of children's court for several minor offences, and spent her days drinking, chain-smoking and sleeping with just about any man who crossed her path.

Florence neither knew nor cared what contraception was. At sixteen she fell pregnant with Ken, one of four unplanned children. Soon after she set her sights on a new paramour, a soldier from Buffalo. The child was an inconvenience that did not fall within their plans, and Ken was made a ward of the state.

Baby Ken began life unloved and unwanted, and things would continue for him in this vein for quite some time. A foster arrangement was found for him with an elderly woman in Rochester, but the woman was indifferent to his care, leaving him with friends and neighbors to be looked after. When the authorities became aware of this, Ken was placed in a new foster home, but it seems this arrangement was not much better than the last. Thus, by the time he was adopted by the Bianchis, he had been passed back and forth between numerous caregivers, who displayed a range of inconsistent reactions to him, from short-lived curiosity to indifference and hostility.

Forensic psychologists believe that the lack of a primary bond with a caregiver in the first three years of life is a common element in the childhood backgrounds of sociopaths and violent criminals. It is also a risk factor for a range of mental disorders in the psychotic and dissociative class.

Young Ken had already had a rough start in life. Was he broken at birth?

Perhaps under the right circumstances, with supportive and nurturing new caregivers, things might have turned out differently. Either way, it didn't much matter, because things in fact were about to get even worse.

The first warning of what lay ahead was the court's hesitancy to award full custody of Ken to the Bianchis. Initially the arrangement was for temporary custody. At this time, Ken was three months old. The court's reasons in delaying fulfillment of the request for full custody are a matter of speculation, but the discharge records from Rochester Hospital where Ken was briefly admitted in 1958 contain a note stating the attending doctor's view that the delay may have been due to questions about the Bianchi's' fitness as parents. Full custody was finally awarded when Ken reached one year of age, much to Frances' relief. From the beginning she was passionately attached to Ken as an antidote to her own feelings of emotional insecurity, and with only temporary custody, she feared he could be snatched from her at any time.

A further ill omen was the fact that the Bianchis had at one time had two other young children in their care under a fostering arrangement, but these children had been removed from the home by the welfare agency. The discharge records from Rochester Hospital noted that the Society for the Prevention of Cruelty to Children was "aware" of Frances' activities and that Frances had taken care of other children, but they had been taken from her for reasons unknown.

Then there was the family's financial situation, and all its consequences. Nicholas was in the unfortunate habit of gambling away his wages at the tracks, and the family was continually on the move trying to evade angry creditors who threatened to kill him. Before Ken reached adolescence he would move residences and schools multiple times. This was a chaotic, unstable home environment, no matter what good intentions may have existed.

Frances had wanted to be a good mother—that much seems self-evident. She was socially ambitious and concerned to be seen doing the right thing. She lined the walls of their cramped apartment at the corner of Broad and Saxon in red chinoiserie wallpaper, and had Ken's room painted in bright hues, decked out with a complete set of child's maple furniture. Toys and colorful picture cut-outs were arrayed against one wall. She had clearly envisioned for herself a normal child, and a normal family life. She placed in her home the markers of domestic happiness and fulfillment hoping that somehow that would make it so. She grasped for a conventionality painfully at odds with both of their natures.

The reality that emerged is an example of a narcissistic family system. She obsessively wanted herself to be loved, to be needed, to have another creature be entirely dependent on her. In this way, while appearing to be single-mindedly devoted to Ken's needs, she used him to meet her own.

There was much Frances was unhappy about. But she rarely allowed these thoughts to trouble her mind. She set them to one side and focused on the things she could control. This is an entirely normal, if not always healthy, psychological coping mechanism. In its extreme form, it becomes—in the psychologist's lexicon—repression and denial.

Focusing solely on Ken was a way for France to distract herself from her own problems: the difficulties in her marriage, the family's perpetually chaotic living and financial situation, her own unsatisfied wish to reach a higher stratum in society. All the while, she could appear to be fulfilling a perfectly admirable social role, that of the dedicated mother. The strategy was flawed, however, not only because the problems persisted, but because the pressures on the child became unbearable.

It is possible that Kenneth Bianchi learned at an early age to deal with reality in the way that his mother did. What you dislike, what you cannot tolerate, all the pressures, no matter how unbearable— simply don't give them any conscious acknowledgement.

When entrenched psychological reflexes of denial and repression are paired with abuse, the result, according to some psychological theories, is the phenomenon of splitting. This is when the ego literally shatters, and other identities are created to cope with the abuse and protect or suppress the "core" or original self.

This is mentioned not by way of proof of an argument for Ken's later diagnosis of multiple personality, but rather to demonstrate why the psychiatrists who reviewed the literature on Ken's early life thought the pieces of the puzzle fit together just so.

Chapter 2

In the Bianchi home the days blurred together. Nicholas was away at work and Frances had nothing to absorb her attention but the care of the house, and of course, Ken.

Ken was a screamer. So was Frances. In winter these two were stuck together in a kind of tortured intimacy for endless hours. From dawn until bedtime it was an endless cycle of tantrums and Frances' alternating efforts at succor and discipline.

The union was intense to the point of claustrophobia. Ken was the centre of Frances' entire world. Despite the constant rancor he was, in her eyes, a perfect child. The slightest suggestion of any emotional upset or threat to his wellbeing sent her into a tailspin.

Frances was a hypochondriac and doctor-shopper. Over time she also focused this persistent health anxiety on her son. Any hint of illness in the boy, from a sniffle to a sore throat, sent her scurrying to the doctors to have Ken evaluated. Early on she also learned to isolate Ken from other children, for fear he would catch germs. This pattern continued throughout his childhood, and lengthy absences from school were common. Ken was no doubt very lonely, but the only attention he could get was from his mother, and nothing got her attention more than being sick.

Whilst certain physical findings were made for Ken, the paper trail of Ken's medical visits suggest that doctors thought his illnesses were mostly psychological in origin. Also significant is that practically every report mentions the troubled relationship between mother and child and the impression that Frances herself was a deeply disturbed individual.

At first, Frances was concerned about mild coughing and what appeared to be allergies. She felt that Ken was particularly sensitive to pollutants in the air and tried to keep him indoors. Between 4 December 1951 and 22 May 1952, Frances took Ken, who at this time was less than a year old, to the doctor a total of eight times. The doctor diagnosed a persistent low-grade respiratory infection that was slow to respond to the treatment given, but was satisfied by the improvement, and found that otherwise the child was in good health and was growing strong. Mrs. Bianchi's concern and repeated visits were viewed as excessive and troublesome.

There was a momentary reprieve to the Bianchi's constrained living situation with a move to a larger, more desirable apartment in Saratoga Street. The residential area was safer and more upscale, and had a fenced-in yard. This move was no doubt a welcome one for Frances, who was—aside from her desire to attain a higher social standing—worried about Ken running out onto the road. Unfortunately it was to be rather short lived. The next move, to Los Angeles, was necessitated both by Nicholas' creditors catching up with him and by Frances' ongoing concern about Ken's lungs. He had by now developed asthma, and she thought a warmer climate would be beneficial. The family went to stay with France's sister, Jennifer Buono—Angelo Buono's mother.

The record of doctor's visits continued in California. Frances took Ken to the Children's Hospital, Los Angeles for multiple complaints including night sweats, bed-wetting and laryngitis. A note in the medical record makes a rather blunt assessment of Frances: "Mother needs help".

During their time in Los Angeles, Ken was enrolled at the Century Park Elementary School, where at the age of five he sustained a fall on a jungle gym. Although Ken sustained no apparent serious injury, the Bianchis—showing a litigious streak—filed suit with the school for $5,000, on the grounds that they had failed in their duty of care.

Following this accident, a new, more troubling set of symptoms appeared. Ken had had previous issues with bedwetting that now turned into day-long incontinence: Ken was forever dribbling urine in his pants, and now Frances imposed the additional humiliation of making him wear sanitary napkins to prevent him soiling his clothes. The introduction of the sanitary napkin regime had apparently been preceded by an incident in a flower shop. Mother and son were standing in the queue to the counter with several other customers when Ken suddenly lost control and peed his pants right then and there in the store.

Frances, according to Ken, berated him loudly in front of all the other patrons and insisted he wear the sanitary napkins thereafter.

In his sixth or seventh year, Ken also began to have petit mal seizures. Sometimes referred to as "absence seizures", these are episodes of short duration where normal consciousness is lost, usually accompanied by a blank stare or upward roll of the eyes, and minor twitching or tics. They can occur both within and outside of epileptic syndromes, and can include automatism, with the subject performing movements that they later have no memory or awareness of; walking to another room for example.

Ken would now go into bizarre trance states in which his eyes would roll back, his head would move from side to side in a repetitive purposeless motion, and he would lose awareness of his surroundings.

Frances decided Ken must be suffering from epilepsy, and took him once again to the doctors to have the new symptoms evaluated. A doctor's letter dated 12 August 1957 recorded that physical examinations and tests had indicated that there was no evidence of involvement of the central or peripheral nervous system in the episodes of eye-rolling and the purposeless movements. It "apparently occurs when the child is frightened or possibly it is a habit which the child developed to attract attention."

The doctor was suggesting that Ken's "physical" problem was in fact a reaction to something in his environment: something unhealthy. The eye rolling occurred when he was "frightened", or when he was "seeking attention". Frances was again sent away empty-handed, without a concrete diagnosis of what was wrong with her perfect little boy, and she was angry.

Frances framed the issue as one of incompetence on the part of the doctors. There was something wrong with Ken, something physically wrong. He was a sick child. But they were too lazy and stupid to figure out what it was and give him the appropriate treatment.

As one doctor would later point out, in her relentless search for an organic diagnosis, it was as if she was at pains to absolve herself of what the doctors seemed to be quietly accusing her of: being a bad mother and the architect of a budding hysteric.

* * *

The eye-rolling and petit-mal seizures continued, peaking during times of acute emotional stress. The time in California had apparently not been happy for anyone, and as soon as Nicholas had saved enough money, the family moved back to Rochester. It seemed that nothing much worked out for the Bianchis. Theirs was a life of false starts and circular efforts, all underpinned by the grand scheme of unsatisfied ambition.

On the drive back east there were violent thunderstorms. Ken went into a panic; from the front seat Frances was not able to calm him and the screaming tantrum gave way to the characteristic withdrawal of consciousness, rocking, shaking and severe eye-rolling.

Soon after this incident there was, by Frances' accounts to medical staff, a precipitate deterioration of all symptoms. Ken's urinary incontinence also worsened. According to a report Frances provided to a doctor Ken now "dribbled" six or seven times a day between morning and bedtime. With the family again settled in Rochester and Ken re-enrolled at school, the soiling problem increased not only Frances' obsessive worry and interference but Ken's isolation from his peers. The other children would laugh at him and bully him about always "peeing his pants". Frances was livid at the teachers and the school administration for allowing this to happen, and had yet another reason to keep him out of class.

In December of 1958 Ken—now aged seven—was admitted to Rochester General Hospital to have the cause of his incontinence investigated. The hospitalization would prove to be an extremely taxing experience for all concerned,; especially the staff.

At first, all seemed to go well. Ken complied with all instructions without comment or complaint. The staff found him well-behaved, perhaps to a degree that suggested he was intimidated by adults and authority figures. He was startled by any loud noise, commotion or aggressive talking; his twitches and tics recurred sporadically when interacting with the nurses. The general impression gained was that this was such a very anxious child.

The following comment is recorded in the write-up of the preliminary physical examination: "quiet and apprehensive seven-year-old ... continually makes purposeless movements of head and hands. The child is polite and appears somewhat passive."

There was a drastic change in Ken's demeanor during visiting hours, when Frances arrived. Suddenly he would have one complaint after another. Tantrums and aggressive outbursts alternated with fits of crying. Mrs. Bianchi would pursue and berate any nurse or doctor within radius for a solution tofor Ken's issue of the moment. If the staff did not jump to accommodate Frances' barrage of demands and questions she became irate. Do something, she demanded. Why wouldn't they just do something? They were incompetent. They were useless. They were all just after her money, and even with that they couldn't do their job.

On the second day of Ken's hospitalization, the staff's trials worsened. The child's fluids had been restricted in order to perform an IVP, an x-ray examination of the entire urinary tract. Frances wasn't happy. Kenneth was accustomed to having plenty of water and this had been part of the management plan for his problems until that time. She threatened to discharge Ken from the hospital prematurely. The chief medic in charge of Ken's care, Dr. Townsend, was eventually—with some difficulty—able to persuade her to have Ken stay so the IVP could be completed.

During further medical examinations at Rochester General, it was discovered that Ken had a congenital deformation of the kidneys known as Horseshoe Kidney. In this condition the kidneys are fused together at one end, creating the characteristic shape of a horseshoe. Nonetheless, the medical staff felt that the urinary dribbling had more to do with emotional upset. The fact that it occurred during the day, not at night, suggested atypical incontinence likely associated with stress. Dr. Townsend referred in his notes to the "complicated psychiatric environment" presented by the mother and child and said he strongly doubted that she would accept any but an organic cause for Ken's problem.

The staff had additional reason to speculate about trouble at home. Frances at one point made the troubling disclosure that she had tried all manner of physical punishments to get Ken to stop wetting. She had spanked him before he went to the toilet in hopes he would "go enough" so that he would not dribble later; but it "hadn't helped".

The likely reality of physical, as well as emotional abuse is alluded to in a note recorded by Dr. Townsend on 17 December 1958: "she uses questioning of the boy to test the accuracy of the house-staff, saying 'He's been whipped when he lies so he wouldn't lie to me'."

But things were about to get even stranger. When Frances learned that the nurses had asked Ken to wash up and take care of himself after visiting the toilet, she went ballistic. She said that she always "took care of Ken herself" when he visited the bathroom. When it was pointed out that it was normal for a boy of his age to be independent in his toileting, she became hysterical. She said that she didn't intend that he should take care of himself, and that she would take care of him "until she was unable to do so physically".

The staff were horrified by this revelation. To them, it raised the possibility that Frances' intrusiveness and domination over every facet of the child's life extended to the inappropriate handling of Ken's genitals. Was Frances' habit of "assisting" Ken in the toilet an indirect form of sexual abuse? What else, then, might be going on, for example at bath time?

The medical investigations into Ken's urinary incontinence had involved the insertion of a catheter into the urethra via the penis, and extensive handling of his genitals and surrounding areas. There is the wider question of how all this, in combination with the mother's inappropriate touching, was experienced by the child. The psychiatrists who evaluated Ken in Washington would touch on the potential significance of this in the later psychopathology of their patient in their reports to Judge Kurtz, observing the fairly obvious correlation between sexual abuse at the hands of the maternal caregiver and Ken's later pervasive hatred and mistrust towards women.

Whatever the truth of all this, the staff at Rochester General Hospital were disturbed enough by what they had seen to recommend psychiatric evaluation and treatment for both Frances and Ken. Frances staunchly refused. Insisting that Ken's problems were a result of organic causes that the doctors had not uncovered due to their own incompetence, she was adamant that she would not allow any psychiatric examination or care for Kenneth until she herself decided this was essential. At every turn she defended her total and complete ownership of the child and any decisions affecting his welfare.

The recommendation for psychiatric evaluation was the final nail in the coffin of relations between Frances and the staff, and much to their frustration, on the day following the IVP exam, Frances signed Ken out of the hospital against advice and consent. Dr. Townsend wrote a lengthy addenda to the discharge summary to protect the hospital's interests in view of the fact that Ken had been discharged early against advice, when they had not completed all physical examinations. Within this report Townsend placed some emphasis upon the fact that the family had been known to social services and many physicians across the country, that two children had already been removed from Mrs. Bianchi's care, and that it seemed obvious that psychological evaluation and help for the mother and child was necessary alongside any physical interventions but that all such help had been refused.

"The relationship between this boy and his mother leaves a lot to be desired … In brief, the relationship between these two might be considered pathological".

* * *

Although it wasn't the primary purpose of Ken's visit, the doctors at Rochester General Hospital had also been troubled by the strange purposeless movements of his hands and face. Finding no organic explanation for the movements, the hospital staff put them down to a stress reaction, possibly of an extreme nature.

Medical and psychiatric literature points to such purposeless movements as a feature of several conditions including dissociation and catatonic schizophrenia. Psychiatrist Ralph Allison would later note that they are often observed in Multiple Personality Disorder patients. Where children are exposed to repeated trauma, the brain systems become sensitized and habituated. A typical pattern is the emergence of a state of hyperarousal; or, in extreme cases, dissociation. Emotional signs are anxiety, vigilance, irritability and impulsivity and characteristic physical signs are musculo-skeletal rigidity and random, purposeless movement. These were the signs Ken presented to several doctors over the years, who repeatedly described him in terms such as "anxious", "apprehensive", and "hyperactive".

Dissociation is a means of fleeing the source of trauma through a kind of psychic withdrawal. It is much more dangerous to the mind and ego than the usual "flight or fight" reaction, in which a person is in a condition of nervous arousal, but remains in a state of realistic self expression.

Later, psychiatrists would wonder if it were possible that Ken, at only six years of age, was already exhibiting signs of extreme trauma reaction and dissociation—well before an integrated identity had even had a chance to develop.

Chapter 3

Whatever horrors a child is subjected to at home, relationships with others—proxy caregivers—in the extended family or community might at least provide a modicum of stability and offset some of the damage.

For Ken this was never a real possibility, as the family was continually on the move. Between 1958 and 1960 they uprooted no less than four times: from rather shabby accommodations in Lyell Avenue in what was then the red-light district of Rochester, to a more upscale pink-painted house on Wildwood Drive in Greece, then on to Villa and Campbell Streets, back in the central area of Rochester.

All this time Ken was also changing schools, and any relationships he might develop with peers and teachers were each time abruptly severed.

Ken later said that he had, in a manner of speaking, devised his own solution to his lack of friends and companionship. Around this time, at eight or nine years of age, he said he began to receive visits from an imaginary friend, whom he called Sticks.

Ken referred to him as a brother or a twin. He appeared to him when he was hiding under his bed from Frances during one of her rages.

Imaginary friends are common in the histories of MPD patients, although they are hardly unusual among psychologically healthy people.

Sticks was initially Ken's playmate, characterized as kind, fun and trustworthy; but over time, Ken said, he changed, and turned "nasty".

Could Sticks have been the progenitor of the malignant Steve?

* * *

Unsurprisingly, with the many moves, Frances' habit of keeping Ken home from school, and his many emotional and behavioral problems, Ken's academic performance was poor. Even so, some of Ken's teachers later described him as a creative child. Strengths in art and writing were noted, though the subject matter of many of his creations—such as the statue with the monster's face found in his basement in Bellingham—were thought rather strange.

Ken, in his early years, was particularly fond of drawing. One of his earliest sketches was a picture of a man with a hat holding a gun: a police officer. It seems that from a tender age, he had developed a fascination with the archetype of the cop, and all the associated themes of power, control and authority.

Ken's teachers felt that his failure to thrive was a result of problems at home, and in a written report, the finger was pointed squarely at Frances. Following a parent-teacher conference on 16 December 1958, the Greece School District made the following note in Ken's file:

"Mrs. Bianchi is in. She is a very nervous person, easily upset. As a result Ken is also nervous and wets his pants. Check his health record. Mother needs to be calmed down."

Frances was fed up with the continual moves and the substandard accommodations. Her dream had always been for middle-class domestic security, so in 1959 she finally persuaded Nicholas to purchase a large, comfortable house in the respectable suburb of Greece, Rochester. The house was well beyond the family's means, and Nicholas was forced to take on extra work hours to finance the mortgage. Social workers affiliated with Rochester Hospital remarked on the obvious irrationality of the decision.

The reality was that the Bianchis could not afford the house. Nicholas's overtime wasn't enough to compensate for their increased expenses, and it wasn't long before the family could neither pay their bills nor meet the mortgage repayments. The Bianchis lost their home and were back living in shabby rentals in central Rochester. Frances' efforts to place them in higher social standing had met with financial disaster.

Things were about to get worse for the Bianchis, however. In 1960 they were reported again to the Society for the Prevention of Cruelty to Children over concerns about Ken's home life. It isn't recorded who made this report, but there is a good chance it was Ken's school. Ken's troubled emotional state was drawing attention and was seen as a red flag of abuse.

Social workers visited the Bianchis on a number of occasions over the next period. The investigation report heavily criticized Frances' dominance and Nicholas' passivity in matters of discipline. The SPCC pointed out that the family's financial situation was a result of the father allowing himself to "pushed around" by the mother. The agency's conclusion was that Frances was "a deeply disturbed person". Without intervention from Nicholas or anybody else outside the family she had "smothered the child in medical attention and maternal concern" from the time of adoption, all of which had distorted Ken's development and led to his tantrums, aggression, wetting and hysterical acting out.

The recommendation for psychiatric assessment and treatment for Frances and the child was again made and again refused. Despite this, Ken was not removed from Frances' care.

One consequence of the dive in the family's fortunes was that Frances herself now went out to work, taking a part-time job with the Bell Aircraft Company. Arrangements were made with a neighbor for Ken's care while she was away from the house, and the social worker from the SPCC noted that during this time Ken's mood and behavior were markedly improved. His urinary incontinence also, for a time, resolved. Nonetheless, the SPCC were now aware that no follow-up had been organized to finalize testing on Ken's kidneys after he had earlier been prematurely discharged from the hospital, so their visits prompted a further round of medical investigations, this time at Strong Memorial Hospital.

The medical staff there, after further intrusive testing and probing, no doubt frightening and painful for Ken, came to the conclusion that there was nothing organically wrong with him to cause the chronic wetting. Ken's problem, they said, was emotional, not physical.

The report of this admission emphasized Frances' defiance towards the doctors and her conviction that they were against her and Ken in every matter. She had relentlessly "doctor-shopped" over the years in search of one that would tell her what she wanted to be told and do what she wanted done, but they always came to the same conclusion: that she was the problem. Dr. Dane Pugh was of the opinion that Frances' history of consulting with doctors about Ken indicated "apparent paranoid trends". He, like the others, recommended psychiatric evaluation for herself and Ken.

Frances was infuriated and insulted by the recommendation for psychiatric treatment and the insinuation that she was the cause of Ken's problem. These medical men impugned her motherhood, the only real purpose and point of pride in her existence. She decided to keep on the search and take her business elsewhere; and, still with no organic diagnosis and Ken's wetting problem continuing unabated, by the end of 1960 she had had enough.

Finally, after consulting with doctors at the Genesee Hospital, she was able to find one willing to perform a procedure that would supposedly correct Ken's incontinence.

Ken was admitted on 28 November. The hospital records indicate that a cystoscopy and retrograde pyelogram under general anaesthesia were performed for diagnostic purposes, revealing the bladder was normal except for mild hypertrophy and "a very slight but definite contracture at the vesicle neck." The pyelogram confirmed the existence of a horseshoe kidney. The hospital performed a meatotomy followed by "periodic urethral dilatations."

A meatotomy is a highly invasive procedure with a painful recovery. It involves cutting of constrictions of the urethra at the tip of the penis and splitting of the underside of the glans. Once again this involved handling, probing and now outright incision and assault on this young boy's genitals.

It is hard to imagine how all this was experienced by a nine-year old boy. At any rate, the operation was not a success, for the incontinence continued. This was unsurprising since the procedure was designed to correct a physical problem, but it had already been observed on numerous occasions that Ken's wetting followed an emotional pattern and came on with anxiety and upset, conditions which were positively unrelenting for him under Frances' care.

It must be said that, even though partial excuse due to Frances' own ignorance and emotional instability may be made, this unnecessary operation on a child of nine years age was a heinous act.

Chapter 4

That there was something distinctly wrong with this child and this family escaped few who came into contact with the Bianchis.

In 1962 they were once again reported to the authorities, this time by the Monsignor at Ken's school. The report referred to concerns over Ken's behavioral problems, difficulties getting along with classmates and teachers, and his chronic absenteeism. Much to Frances' chagrin, she and Ken were now referred to the DePaul psychiatric clinic, whose reports would later be of such interest to Bianchi's defense team. With social services threatening her, Frances finally—and reluctantly—complied.

The two visited the clinic twice, and the staff there made extensive notes of their observations of this decidedly toxic relationship.

The DePaul reports repeat themes set out in the earlier medical literature but give a darker and more disturbing insight into the mother-son relationship. Presumably, over time, that relationship had grown deeper and more enmeshed, and not in a good way.

But Ken was also reaching pre-adolescence, and now there were suggestions that the relationship had an inappropriately sexual tenor.

In the consultation rooms, Frances allegedly comported herself seductively, stroking her leg and frequently pulling down her blouse to reveal more of her bosom. She struck the doctor as threatening, critical and overly involved where Ken was concerned, "having her own needs met with the son". During the consultations he learned she had hit Ken with a shower hose and shown him sex magazines. There were "oedipal problems, with the mother provocative and wanting love".

A Dr. Dowling prepared the report that would later become fodder for speculations about an MPD diagnosis.

He concluded that Kenneth was both very hostile and very dependent. He depended on Frances for his very survival, therefore he kept his great anger under cover, through a massive effort of repression and denial which caused obvious strain on his whole personality and development. The denial was to such an extent he had told Dr. Dowling that his mother and father were "the best parents in the world."

Kenneth was, in Dowling's view, extremely lonely and wanted to move away from Frances and towards other relationships; but he was limited by Frances and feared hurting, and being hurt by, her, should he strive for greater independence.

He expended great effort in pleasing Frances, but she was never happy with him. Dowling's conclusion about Ken's medical issues was that these were psychosomatic complaints, and they were the only means by which he could get back at his mother. Without them, the doctor concluded on a note of irony, he might well have been "a severely disturbed child".

Dowling felt strongly that Frances Bianchi was not motivated to get help for herself or for Ken. After the second visit to the DePaul Clinic, Frances bluntly refused any more assessment or treatment for Ken, effectively sealing a fate that seemed already predestined.

* * *

The figure of Nicholas in this story is notable mainly for his absence. Yet it is clear from Kenneth Bianchi's later recollections that he adored and idealized his father.

Ken would always positively compare Nicholas with Frances; where she was shrill and aggressive—"always yelling"—Nicholas was friendly, helpful and kind. Perhaps with Nicholas away from the home so much for work, Ken was able to fill in the blanks, and fantasize an ideal loving parent.

Ken later recalled that around twelve years of age he grew much closer to his father, and moved away from Frances somewhat. Psychiatrists speculated that there might have been an opportunity here for Ken to recoup some emotional normality, and possibly for things to turn out differently. But the budding relationship was to be cut short.

Always writ large in Ken Bianchi's later memories of his father was the fishing trip the two took together, one of the few times they had spent substantial time alone without Frances present.

Ken, now poised on adolescence, had grown to the point where he and his father fit the same shoe size, and the two had purchased identical dress shoes.

Ken was enamored of the new shoes and wanted to take them on the fishing trip. Nicholas did not have anything to say about it; if Ken wanted the lovely shoes with him then so be it.

Ken had a pair of old sand shoes and the dress shoes with him. He kept them separate so the dress shoes would not get muddy. Ken recalled that he and his father had a wonderful time on this expedition, getting to know each other free from Frances' intrusion.

When Ken and Nicholas returned home from the trip, Ken realized to his dismay that he had left the dress shoes behind. There was a plan in place to return and look for the shoes; but then something else, something unexpected happened.

A couple of days later Ken and Frances were at home while Nicholas was away at work. A knocking came at the door. Frances went to open it and there were two police officers standing on the porch.

Nicholas had suffered a massive heart attack while at work. In his efforts to keep the family afloat amidst their worsening financial situation, he had literally toiled his way into an early grave.

When Ken found out he came completely undone: screamed for hours, balling his fists and hyperventilating. He could not be calmed. He fled to his room, where he would spend a lot of time alone over the next period.

Following Nicholas' death, accounts state that Ken withdrew from Frances and other relatives who came to visit and pay respects and condolences. He hid away in his bedroom or the attic, often with the lights out, crying and talking to his lost father. He wanted nothing to do with the family and would not be consoled by them.

When it came time to attend the funeral, Ken remembered the dress shoes he had left behind on the fishing trip with his father. Due to his carelessness he now had no appropriate shoes to wear to the funeral.

It isn't clear whose idea it was—Ken's, Frances' or the funeral director's—but in the end Nicholas' dress shoes were removed from the body as the corpse's legs were hidden under the half-open casket, and Ken himself wore his father's shoes to the funeral.

As practical as this solution might have been there was something odd about it, something psychologically unpleasant. Ken was grieving his dead father; wearing his clothes, especially so soon after the death, was not something that could be regarded as particularly healthy in that process.

* * *

Ken now had nobody in the world except Frances, and in one sense her control and influence over the child was without challenge. But things were also changing.

One has to wonder if subconsciously, he blamed Frances for Nicholas' death, and added this to the tally of buried resentments against his mother. As dependent as he was on her, this was a major blow to their relationship, and he had new impetus to throw off the yoke of her control in whatever way he could.

He was growing into adolescence, becoming something approximating a man. Now, many of the physical problems that plagued him through childhood gradually resolved. His psychological and emotional problems however remained unaddressed; growing sophistication and systems of impression management merely better concealed them. More worryingly, they now fused with his budding sexuality.

The ingredients were all perfectly in place for the disastrous person he would become.

Chapter 5

Ken began high school in late 1965. Initially he was admitted to the McQuaid Jesuit High School, but his tenure there would only last a short time. In 1967 he enrolled at Gates-Chili High, where he would complete his studies and finally graduate, but with little distinction. Reports from Gates-Chili evince a continuation of earlier patterns—poor academic performance and lengthy and frequent absences. Ken tried hard to make friends, observed one school report, but he "needed to learn more acceptable ways". They put down his emotional problems to a less than ideal home environment.

Despite Ken's poor scholastic record, there was a certain transformation taking place. He had grown into a handsome young man. Always tidy and well-groomed, he wore his hair short, unlike the more rebellious students, and was polite and deferential to his elders. Ken's picture from the graduation yearbook evinces the smiling, all-American, clean-cut kid with a twinkle in his eye.

In this carefully maintained image of blandness and conformity, Ken found an ideal cover to indulge his true desires. Whilst Ken made few friends at Gates-Chili, a co-educational High School with teenagers coming from a range of backgrounds, he had greater opportunities to develop a new and more compelling interest: girls.

Already, there was a record of him getting into trouble for inappropriate behavior. According to the reports of the DePaul Clinic, at age twelve he had taken a six-year-old girl's pants down. This event had been a source of shame and anxiety to Frances, but the staff at the clinic concluded that she, to a degree, provoked his sexual acting out by intrusive "prying".

According to one account, Ken Bianchi was sexually active from the age of eleven. A confession is allegedly recorded in which he described his first sexual encounter with a blonde "woman", described as slim and "easy to speak with" with a beguiling manner of "flirting", her head tilted to the side. The "woman" in the account was in fact only nine years old.

The tale reads like a romance novel: Ken's hands shook due to nerves but he tried his best to be patient and gentle, and "just held her" when he was finished. It was, according to the account, the most beautiful and memorable experience of his life until that time.

Ken allegedly stated that he enjoyed two further encounters with this "woman", but they didn't go steady because she was involved with several other guys in the area. If true, this is intriguing. Ken Bianchi not only attributes a pre-adolescent girl with all the traits of a grown woman, but projects on her the so-called "Madonna/Whore" complex: on the one hand she is romanticized, deserving of being treated with patience and care; on the other she is not worthy of his steady affections because she is merely the tramp around town.

Ken attributed his scholastic problems mostly to the distractions of girls. He was crazy about "women" and dated many different ones on a regular basis.

One of these was an eleven-year old girl called Sue Davis. The account of their "break up" is intriguing. Sue invited Ken to a pool party at her place along with other teenagers. Ken "unintentionally" brushed against Sue's breast in the pool. She became upset at him, feeling he had touched her without her permission, an allegation which upset him greatly. This story raises an interesting question about the workings of Kenneth Bianchi's mind and his propensity to lie not only to others but to himself. Were Sue and Ken really "dating", or was this simply his way of framing predatory actions against girls so that he appeared to be the innocent party?

It seems that in all Ken's talk of the various "women" he dated and enjoyed encounters with at this time, he is oftentimes speaking of under-aged girls. And it appears that while Ken chose women closer to his own age for formal "dates" and public respectability, his predilection for teenagers and pre-teen girls continued throughout his life, and was to become a recurring theme.

A little girl was never going to control Ken, make demands or bring him to heel. He would always be in charge. After all he had suffered at the hands of his mother, such was surely a potent lure.

* * *

At Ken's school, he said, there were the easy types who would get around with any guy just for fun. Then there were the "good girls" who were waiting for marriage. Ken had his fair share of the former type but, like his mother, he already had a rather naïve vision of a certain kind of idyllic family future for himself, always imagining that he would take the most beautiful and morally pure kind of woman as a wife.

During his senior years at Gates-Chili, he met a young stunner named Brenda Beck. She checked all the boxes. She was flawless looking, sweet and submissive—or so Ken thought.

The two entered into a hasty marriage in 1971, shortly after Ken's graduation. They had certain important things in common, but nothing that could really bring them together. Both were extremely young (Ken at this time was only 19), and both had over-involved and meddling mothers, who they would turn to for advice and support during the rocky course of the union, far more than they would to each other.

It turned out that they differed sharply in what they were expecting from the union. Ken wanted to immediately settle into the role of husband and provider, and for Brenda to settle into the role of wife and homemaker. A house and children would not be far behind. It turned out that Brenda, although she was willing to commit to marriage in the formal sense, still wanted to explore life like any young person. She wanted to leave the house when she liked, have her own friends and do things that didn't always revolve around Ken. It wasn't long before his demands chafed on her.

Another issue was Ken's jealousy, which was to become a recurring motif in his relationships. Ken resented Brenda's profession as a nurse, and was concerned that Brenda would fall into the arms of one of the many patients or doctors she interacted with on a daily basis. He also held a grudge about her intimacy with another man previous to the marriage, and had accused her of having an affair with his own supervisor.

The newlyweds fought often about these issues and others, and with the marriage already disintegrating before Ken's eyes, he initiated a campaign to woo Brenda back. He sent her flowers and wrote her poems, courtship rituals he would employ over the years with many women with varying degrees of success.

Brenda was not impressed and took these tokens as a mark of Ken's shallowness and immaturity. He seemed to live in a dream world, thinking that if he robotically performed the appropriate romantic actions and said the right things at the right moments, everything would work out in his favor. It didn't.

The marriage ended within the year. Ken's version had it that he returned home one day to find the apartment empty and cleared of furniture. Brenda had taken off, taking most of their possessions with her. Another says that Brenda found Ken in bed with another woman, one Janice Duschong, and threw him out.

Nobody knows for sure which story is true. What is clear is that Ken's stories about his past, particularly where women were concerned, tended to paint himself as the victim, when the reality was that he was chronically unfaithful. Not only did he habitually date several women at once, he also visited prostitutes in Rochester—certainly once he had graduated, but probably even before then.

Ken's romantic and sexual habits were not all that unusual for young men of his time and place—perhaps just a little more indulgent and extreme. The seventies was the beginning of the era of mass commercialized sex. Suddenly sex, in whatever form you wanted it—call girls, street hookers, dirty magazines, porn movies, swingers clubs and key parties—was available everywhere, and compared to earlier times, relatively free of stigma.

* * *

Ken's professional efforts after leaving school did not fare much better than his marriage. Perhaps the only thing in his favor was that from very early on, he had a clear idea of what he wanted to be: a police officer.

In 1970 he enrolled at Monroe County Community College to study police science. He also undertook courses in psychology, a budding sphere of interest that would prove to be of great use to him in the only "career" that he would eventually pursue with any real application or interest.

Despite the limited attention he gave his studies, Ken was gaining a C average. But this wasn't in any way satisfactory to him. The delusional force of his narcissism persuaded him that he should excel with little effort, but the reality was that he was an ordinary scholar at best.

The following year, Ken was so disappointed with his exam results that he decided to drop out. So it was that in 1971 Ken, his marriage over and his professional plans in tatters, moved back home and found himself once again alone with his mother—apart from Frances' cat, a white shorthair.

They lived together at 105 Glendale Park, in the Edgerton district of Rochester. Ken plodded forward, finding casual work as a mobile ice-cream and snack vendor. He had a car, some pocket money, and relative freedom; but he was bitterly disappointed at how his life was turning out.

Frances Bianchi told one interviewer in the 1990s that Ken reacted very badly indeed to stress and misfortune.

It seemed that every time he broke up with a girl, the interviewer reported she'd said, he'd go out and kill somebody.

Chapter 6

The town of Churchville in Monroe County is roughly six miles from Chili, where Ken Bianchi attended high school, and within a few miles radius of Edgerton, where Ken was, in 1971, living with his mother.

On 18 November 1971, two young boys were dirt biking in the rural area between Churchville and the outskirts of nearby Riga when they came upon the dead body of a pre-adolescent girl lying on the slope of a ditch. Naked but for her sweater and socks, she had been raped and strangled.

She was ten-year old Carmen Colon, a Puerto Rican immigrant who had been living for several years with various family members in the greater Rochester area.

Carmen had lain undiscovered in the ditch outside Riga for some forty-eight hours.

Two days previous, she left her mother's house on Romeyn Street in the late afternoon and headed towards the Jax Drugstore in the shopping complex on the corner of West Main and Genesee Streets, just a five-minute walk from the house. There she was seen by the pharmacist, who told her it would take around half an hour to process the prescription her mother had given her. Carmen left the store, telling him she would return in a while to collect the drugs. She never did.

Exactly what happened after that is a mystery. But the pharmacist was not the last bystander to see Carmen alive. In the days following the murder, three witnesses came forward and told police that around five on the evening of Carmen's disappearance, they had seen a young girl, naked from the waist down, running alongside the Interstate 490 West. The witnesses said Carmen was being pursued by a dark-haired man in an off-white colored sedan.

Effectively, what they had seen was a desperate but unsuccessful attempt at escape. Carmen had been abducted, snatched into a vehicle, and had managed to get out and make a break for it down the freeway.

She ran as hard as she could, the sound of engines roaring behind her and the scent of burning oil in her nostrils. There was plenty of traffic; she should have had every reasonable prospect of rescue. It is highly unlikely that the three witnesses were the only motorists to have seen her. But her killer had caught up with her, because of all the cars that passed by that afternoon, sadly, not a one stopped.

The papers vented community outrage and decried the collapse of moral standards and crowd apathy:

'No one stopped!'

'Apathy Abounds as Motorists Ignore Girl'

'Nobody Stopped to Save Carmen'

'Girl is Slain after Motorists Ignore her Pleading for Help'

'Hundreds Saw Carmen, No Motorist Stopped'

These were bitter times. Rochester natives sighed about what was happening to their beloved city. Maybe it had grown too big, too transient; there were too many strangers. On 21 November 1971, alarm swelled when the *Democrat and Chronicle* reported that graffiti had been discovered in the men's washroom at Sibley, Lindsay and Curr Department Store, a couple of miles from the home of Carmen's grandparents. Somebody had scrawled on the back of the wooden cubicle door: "I killed a 10-year old girl. Who will be next?"

* * *

There was an unusual discovery when tests were run on Carmen's clothing. Cat fur, off white in color, was found. None of Carmen's relatives owned a cat. The coroner wondered whether the cat fur had been transferred from the clothing of Carmen's killer.

The police made another important discovery in the Colon murder that they could not yet appreciate the significance of. Tests on semen traces inside the girl's body indicated that the man they were looking for was a non-secretor.

In 1973, after his marriage to Brenda collapsed, Ken was dating around, often more than one girl at a time. One woman he was involved with was Janice Duschong, who, according to one version of events, Brenda had sprung him in bed with, prompting her to dissolve the union.

Ken's methods of courtship were traditional and laced with syrupy romance. He sent Janice flowers and wrote her poetry and letters. Janice received one letter from Ken that would later pique the interest of the Rochester authorities. In it he claimed that he had already killed someone, and that he was sure he was a suspect in their murder. Ken expressed concern in the letter that a vehicle similar to his own Dodge Dart had been spotted near the dumping site.

Janice laughed off these confessions as wild stories. Ken had always been prone to spout outlandish tales in which he was the hero or villain. It was his way of puffing himself up and impressing the ladies. She never entertained for a moment that he might, for once, be telling the truth.

Janice later recalled that around this time Ken was making a collage. He took a large piece of cardboard and cut out pictures of little girls from magazines and stuck them on the board. She thought it was sweet; Ken had often talked of his love of children.

Ken saw Janice off and on during 1973. Their relationship was never truly committed, but Janice thought she had a good thing going with him. So she was shocked and upset when—history repeating—she found him in bed one day with another young lady, Donna Duranso.

Janice kicked Ken to the curb.

And then, it happened again.

On 3 April 1973, New York state trooper Thomas Zimmer was on patrol along NYS Route 104 in Webster, a suburb of Rochester, when he spotted something that stood out on a hillside sloping down from the Irondequoit Bay rest area. Taking a closer look, he found a pre-teen girl in a blue and white checked dress slumped face down in the dirt. The girl's coat was found on the ground several meters away. Although she had been found clothed, Zimmer was reminded of Carmen Colon. The later autopsy would reveal that Wanda had suffered the same fate: she had been raped and strangled to death.

She was eleven-year-old Wanda Walcowicz who, just a day earlier, had come home from school in a buoyant mood. Although she had missed many days at school that year, she had just received a positive report card from her teacher. The excitement over Wanda's achievement was short lived, however; her mother Joyce said she was out of diapers for little baby Michelle, and sent Wanda out to the store.

Dressed in a coat against the drizzle, and the same dress, white socks and sneakers she had worn to school, Wanda headed out along Avenue D, the same route she had taken to school every day for years without incident. With her flame red hair, she stood out anywhere she went.

Along the way she ran into three school friends, and walked with them as far as the corner of Conkey and Avenue D, before proceeding alone to the grocer, where she was served by store clerk Richard Chechi. He later said that all had seemed normal with Wanda that afternoon. A former Walcowicz babysitter was sitting in Jimmy's Tavern and spotted Wanda walking back along Conkey in the direction of her home. She had considered walking Wanda home, because it was now lightly raining and she had an umbrella, whereas the little girl didn't. She made a split-second decision against it.

But Wanda's luck was about to get worse. The three friends who had accompanied her on the first part of her journey to the store now saw her coming down Conkey, a few blocks behind them. They thought of waiting for Wanda to catch up, but because it was raining they decided to hurry on home.

Looking back down the street, they saw Wanda leaning against a post, trying to get a better handle on her heavy grocery bag. They glanced back again a few moments later—and Wanda was gone.

* * *

An odd finding during the examination of the body was some custard in Wanda's stomach contents. This meant she had consumed the treat within two hours of her death; however she hadn't purchased any custard at the grocer, and she hadn't eaten any at home before she left. Police theorized that she had been given the custard by her killer.

Two detectives from the Monroe County Sherriff's Office who had worked on the Colon case were assigned to the Walcowicz investigation. Suspicions were growing of a connection between the killings. The girls were roughly the same age, both had disappeared running afternoon errands, and both had been sexually assaulted and strangled.

Another connection: testing of Wanda's clothes revealed that they were littered with white-colored cat dander, as Carmen's had been.

Four days after she had disappeared, a funeral service was held at St. Michael's Catholic Church on Clinton Street. Father Benedict Ehmann, alluding to the earlier death of Carmen Colon, called for the "yoke of fear" to be lifted from the neighborhood. The notion that the cases were linked was cemented on 4 April when the *Times-Union* ran a piece observing similarities to the Colon murder.

The police implemented a secret witness program whereby people could anonymously provide tips, and a large reward was posted via the press and town billboards. The leads began pouring in. One caller said that he had seen a red-haired girl forced into a vehicle on the corner of Conkey and Avenue D between half past five and six on the night of Wanda's disappearance. The car, he said, was a white Dodge Dart. Two other callers mentioned seeing a similar vehicle, a light colored Dart, at the rest area at Webster where Wanda's body was dumped.

Around six weeks after Wanda's death, the *Times-Union* announced that despite it being one of the biggest investigations in Monroe County history, the probe was winding down amidst a lack of viable leads.

Officials were no closer to apprehending the killer who may have taken the life of not only Wanda, but Carmen. But detectives weren't entirely sure if the two cases were related, and their hope was that speculation about a serial killer was misplaced.

That is, until five months later, when there was a victim number three.

* * *

On 28 November 1973, a Wayne County fire chief was travelling along Eddy Road in a lonely rural area just outside the town of Macedon, about thirty miles from Rochester. He spotted a body in a ditch off the side of the road, resting on its side, as if it had been tossed out of a vehicle and rolled down the slope.

The girl had been raped and strangled. She was redressed, but the fasteners on her shirt were broken. Her coat, like Wanda's, was found a short distance from her body.

The Wayne County Sherriff's Office was responsible for the investigation into this murder, since it fell inside their county jurisdiction; however as suspicions of a connection between the cases grew, they worked in cooperation with the Rochester PD, the Monroe County Sherriff's Office and now the New York State Police. Wayne County Sherriff Richard Pisciotti photographed the scene and assisted with removal of the body to Newark State Hospital where the girl's father confirmed her identity: Michelle Maenza.

Christopher Maenza left the hospital in tears. Evidence of the brutality of the assault upon Michelle was writ clear upon her body. The autopsy showed extensive bruising on her face, neck and arm. Michelle's neck was crossed by a clear, deep red line, as well as finger marks; it appeared she had been not only strangled with an object—likely a belt—but the killer had additionally used his hands to choke her.

* * *

Eleven-year-old Michelle lived with her mother Carolyn and her younger sisters Marie and baby Christine at 25 Webster Crescent, in the northeast of Rochester. Carolyn worried about her girls being out alone on the streets, and made it a habit to accompany them on foot to and from school each day.

On 26 November 1973, Carolyn arrived in the afternoon as usual to pick up her daughters, but only Marie was waiting for her. She was informed that Michelle had been kept back in school. To Carolyn's mind, Michelle was growing up—it would be her twelfth birthday in a few days; although it wasn't her usual practice, she decided to proceed home alone with Marie. She didn't know how long they would be kept waiting, and surely Michelle could make the short distance home by herself.

Michelle's last day alive wasn't a happy one. The kids at Michelle's school continually taunted her for her chubbiness. She had been kept back in detention with a school bully after another episode of teasing; presumably Michelle had been equally blamed for whatever transpired. She finally left the school around quarter past three, and was seen a short time later by two neighborhood friends, turning from Webster into Ackerman. Michelle therefore was not headed home, but towards the nearby Goodman Plaza. Carolyn had left a purse at the Super Saver store there the previous Saturday. It seems likely there had been some mix up of the family arrangements; Michelle might have thought she was going to meet Carolyn and Marie at the plaza where they were to collect the purse, but Carolyn and Marie had already gone home.

Michelle's uncle Phillip Maenza worked at a gas station along Michelle's route. He later said he saw Michelle that afternoon, and offered her a ride—which she declined.

Around five, when Michelle still had not returned home, Carolyn panicked. She called the Rochester Police and reported Michelle missing. A description of the girl was broadcast over patrol car radios: shoulder length dark brown hair, wearing a long purple coat, knee-high black boots and purple slacks with a zigzag pattern. Within hours a full search of the northwest districts was in operation. When that turned up nothing, a countywide investigation was set in motion. The police however could not have known that Michelle's abductor had already crossed the county border with his victim.

There were reports that a girl matching Michelle's description had been seen at the Goodman Plaza entrance around 3:30 pm. Another tip concerned a sighting of a frightened girl who looked like Michelle in the passenger seat of an off-white sedan travelling down Browncroft Boulevard, five minutes east of Webster Avenue, at around 5:40 pm.

Despite the fact that, like Wanda and Carmen, she had been spotted by numerous witnesses—even members of her own family—people who, had they appreciated the danger, could have stepped in to help, she had been swiftly and quietly whisked away into the darkness, her fate a mystery until she was found cold and motionless in an earthen grave.

Whoever was responsible was a stealthy, invisible and seemingly practiced predator.

* * *

A finding of interest during the autopsy was the remains of a cheeseburger inside Michelle's stomach. Here again were echoes of the Walcowicz murder. Like Wanda, Michelle had apparently eaten a fast food item within hours of her death, although—like Wanda—she had had no money on her. Was the killer plying his victims with treats?

Now, investigators could see numerous clues connecting this case with the Walcowicz case, as well as—perhaps more remotely—the Colon murder. All three girls, of Roman-Catholic background, had disappeared while running late afternoon errands for their mothers. All were similar ages, on the cusp of adolescence. All had been snatched from the streets in daylight, raped, strangled, and dumped by roadsides. There was no attempt to conceal their bodies. Possibly the killer wanted them to be found, was entertained by the prospect of driving fear into the community, or enjoyed toying with the investigators, flaunting his boldness.

Forensic examination of Michelle's clothing had again revealed the presence of cat fur, which had also been found on Wanda and Carmen's clothes. Investigators suspected that the man or men they were looking for lived with a white or light colored cat, or even entertained the possibility that he was luring the girls to his car with a cat.

Today, DNA technology would have been able to determine if the fur found on all three victims had come from the same cat, which in turn would have helped to establish whether there was one or more killers involved in the three murders. As it was, a level of uncertainty remained about whether Michelle and Wanda had died at hands of the same man who had killed Carmen. Detectives were fairly confident of a link between the Maenza and Walcowicz cases, but were less sure about Carmen.

Using a new technique involving iodine and silver, detectives were able to lift wrist prints from Michelle's neck. At that time there was nothing to match them to—but they may yet prove valuable in identifying her killer.

* * *

Michelle's birthday fell on 1 December 1973, three days after she was killed. Instead of opening presents and blowing out the candles on her birthday cake, she was lowered into the ground in a casket at Holy Sepulchre Cemetary, where Wanda and Carmen's bodies had also been interred.

Once again a secret witness hotline was set up, and by 1 December, almost 1,500 calls were received. Several tips that came through seemed to recall leads in the earlier cases. A sedan was seen parked on the opposite side of Eddy Road around 5:30 pm on the day Michelle went missing, near where the body was found. Police tried matching the car to a list of similar vehicles registered in Rochester, but came up with no workable leads.

One of Michelle's friends told police that on the Monday afternoon Michelle vanished, she had seen her walking down Ackerman towards Goodman Plaza. As the witness was heading back to Webster Crescent, she said she saw Michelle again, this time in the front seat of a beige car speeding out of Goodman Plaza. The beige vehicle was travelling so fast it nearly crashed into another car that was turning from Webster into Ackerman. Whoever was driving that car wanted to get out of there in a hurry.

Police were later able to locate the driver of the car that had almost collided with the beige vehicle at the intersection of Ackerman and Goodman. There were two other vehicles at the intersection that day, and the drivers of those cars were contacted also. Witness statements collected from this exercise led to the first preliminary physical description of a suspect. He was a white male, of slim build and around six feet tall, with fair-medium skin and dark wavy hair.

A sketch was prepared and distributed to news stations in Monroe and Wayne counties. Following its publication, there was a flurry of calls to the hotlines from witnesses claiming to have seen a man resembling the sketch, and additional investigators were assigned to the case to follow these up.

Authorities thought they had a major break in the case when a motorist came forward describing a troubling encounter with a man on State Route 350 in Macedon that took place on the same day that Michelle was abducted. The motorist told police that he had been driving along Route 350 when he saw an off-white colored vehicle pulled over on the shoulder near the intersection with Eddy Road, the same road on which Michelle's body had been found.

Thinking the driver probably had a flat tire or engine trouble, he pulled over to offer a hand. As he walked towards the vehicle, the driver stepped out, and he noticed that the man was concealing what he described as a "chubby" pre-teen girl behind him. The motorist started to speak, and as he did so the man stepped forward—still hiding the girl behind him—and moved slightly to the side, so he was positioned in front of the license plate, now also hidden from view. The witness recounted that he fled the scene when the man became belligerent, shouting and raising his fist. At that time, he was unaware that any child had been abducted, so he never reported the incident until much later. To authorities, the fact that the man had concealed the license plate raised the question of whether the person they were looking for was an old hand at crime, or someone familiar with police procedure.

After the police sketch was released in the media, a woman called in saying she had seen a man resembling the picture taking a hamburger to a young girl in a car at Carrols Drive-in Restaurant in the Panorama Plaza in Penfield at about 4:30 pm on the day Michelle disappeared. This location was close to the spot where the Route 350 witness had the encounter with the suspicious man. Detectives strongly considered the possibility that this was the same individual, and the proffering of the hamburger to a young girl was another link connecting that sighting to the Maenza murder.

* * *

Police and the public had noticed another, rather bizarre connection in the cases, one with seemingly occult significance. All the victim's names featured double initials: C.C. for Carmen Colon; W.W. for Wanda Walcowicz, and M.M. for Michelle Maenza. If that weren't coincidental enough, these initials also matched the first letter of the name of the township closest to where each body was found: Carmen's body was found near Churchville, Wanda's in Webster, and Michelle's in Macedon.

In time, the unsolved murders of Carmen, Wanda and Michelle would always be popularly referred to as the Double Initial or Alphabet Murders.

Various witnesses who had come forward to make statements in connection with the alphabet murders had described a similar kind of car. It was a light-colored sedan—off white or beige. One witness in the abduction of Wanda had described a white Dodge Dart. The Rochester police never interviewed Bianchi, but had they questioned him about these murders back in the early seventies, they might have been interested to know that he drove this very type of car: a white Dodge Dart.

They might also have been intrigued to know that he lived with a white cat, belonging to his mother, and about his occasional work in this period as a mobile ice cream and snack vendor.

His job was to supply local kids with treats—ice cream and sodas. This fit with the evidence that Wanda and Michelle had consumed a fast food item before they died—in Wanda's case custard; in Michelle's, a cheeseburger. If Bianchi's job involved giving treats to children, he had perhaps learned a handy trick to more easily bend them to his will.

In 1973, when Michelle Maenza was murdered, Ken had been seeing a woman named Donna Duranso. Their relationship collapsed shortly before Michelle was killed. There is an eerie and repeated pattern of coincidence between the dissolution of Ken's relationships and the murders of the alphabet victims.

The people of Rochester were afraid that the alphabet killer would strike again. But he never did. This string of killings stopped not long before Kenneth Bianchi left Rochester for Los Angeles, where another string of strangling murders soon began.

PART TWO:
CALIFORNIA DREAMING

Chapter 7

Since dropping out of college, Ken was adrift in Rochester like garbage floating on the Genessee River. He had meandered through a series of short-term jobs—including the stint as an ice-cream vendor—but had certainly not settled upon anything resembling a career.

For a time he worked nights as an ambulance attendant, a job he told friends he enjoyed, because he "got to help people"—but he couldn't stand the nocturnal shift work. After that he took a job as a bouncer at a nightclub. His explanation for leaving that job was interesting. One night he had been forced to "come down heavy" on a customer. He just couldn't abide violence, so he had quit.

Bianchi's self-image was sharply at odds with the man his actions would later prove him to be. In his narrative, he was a regular guy who just wanted a regular job with normal hours, where he could help people. And he hated aggression or to see anybody hurt.

Despite the bouncer gig not working out, a move into the security business still seemed desirable; it was at least distantly related to his true passion of police work. So Ken was pleased as punch when he managed to score a job as a security officer at J.B. Hunters, a large department store in central Rochester.

The role was steady for a while, but Ken began indulging in a sideline that was to become his downfall in this and many future jobs.

He was nothing if not contradictory. He worked in security and ardently aspired to be a police officer, protecting America from the criminal underclass; but at Hunters he was surrounded by jewelry and other high-end goods, and he just couldn't resist helping himself to a five-finger discount.

Ken wooed his girlfriends, including Susan Moore, a petite and pretty brunette who also worked at Hunters, with the goods he pilfered from the store. Ken and Susan dated on and off, but she was not the least impressed with Ken's generous gifts, often knowing the very counter from which he had taken them.

When Susan pointed out this fact to Ken and called him out on the stealing, she was stunned by his reaction.

He wasn't a thief, he insisted. Even the suggestion was insulting.

—Well where did you get it, then?

Ken fixed her with a stare that could be interpreted as communicating either sincerity or censure.

—Well, I'm not quite sure now, I went to so many different places looking for the right one. But I know I bought it, with my money.

Ken maintained his bold-faced denials even in the face of hard evidence. It was if reality simply did not exist.

* * *

When Ken's thieving caught up with him and he was dismissed from Hunters, he was back to square one. Nothing was working out for him, professionally or romantically.

Susan was continually disappointed by Ken's impractical and opportunistic ways. He had proposed to her, but she declined, citing his irresponsibility and dubious moral character. If the thieving wasn't bad enough, he was also disloyal. Twice, she had caught Ken and Donna Duranso alone together. All in all, Ken had too many strikes against him, and she ended the relationship.

Ken had many love affairs, but they always seemed to go badly. What began with hearts and flowers routinely ended in acrimony.

Smarting from being jilted by Susan, Ken consoled himself again with Donna; but it wasn't long before she, too, cooled things off. To Donna, Ken had always seemed rather sweet, but after she left him, she saw a very different side. Ken turned up at Donna's apartment to "talk things out", but when she tried to send him away, he smashed a window and climbed into the apartment complex.

Donna fled and called the police. They arrested Ken and brought them both back to the station. During processing of the incident, Ken blubbered continuously and kept saying how he didn't know what had come over him. It wasn't like him; he would never do anything like that again. He was just upset because of how much he loved Donna.

Seeing how remorseful and sad Ken was, Donna decided to drop the charges. Their relationship was over, but he had avoided an entry on the rap sheet.

Despite his own possessiveness, Ken felt it entirely unreasonable that any woman he was seeing should hold him to the same standards of fidelity.

He briefly dated another young woman in Rochester named Eve who allegedly "went crazy" on him when she ran into another lady he was seeing at the same time. By now Ken had moved out of Frances' home and into his own apartment, which he had lovingly adorned with a collection of antique mugs. When Eve learned Ken had been two-timing her, she tore up his apartment and trashed the mug collection, pegging the entire set at him one after another. Troubled by the noise, neighbors called the cops. When they arrived, they found Kenny pinning Eve to the floor, by his account, in self-defense.

It didn't matter; it was another incident in which the police had become involved, and by now, Ken was attracting a pile of negative attention in Rochester. As 1975 drew to a close, Ken was unemployed, single, and had a growing list of enemies.

* * *

Ken had been toying with the notion of relocating to California for some time, and now, faced with the prospect of getting through another bleak Rochester winter, he began to entertain the idea more seriously.

There was nothing tying him to his hometown anymore. Not even Frances.

Things had somehow changed between Ken and his mother. She had remarried, and she didn't need him anymore. After all they had been through together, this must have come as quite a shock; when Ken told her he was considering a move west, she began pulling strings and doing everything in her power to help him leave. She got in touch with her sister Jennifer Buono in Los Angeles. Jenny spoke to Angelo, who agreed to give Ken a room until he got on his own feet.

Frances' motives in helping the son she had desperately clung to for so many years to move thousands of miles away, to the other side of the country, are a matter of speculation. It was certainly a radical change of tune on her part. Perhaps it was simply a matter of having transferred her emotional dependency on her son to her new husband. Ken had outlived his use and was discarded.

Or maybe there was more to it than that. There was no doubt that Ken was trouble; of what order of trouble Frances thought he was is unknown. But maybe it was trouble she wanted far away.

For himself, Ken was just another of the many youngsters lured to the west coast by the promise of year-round summer and bigger, better things. California beckoned like an idyll, like the dream destination promised by a thousand postcards and billboards, synonymous with Hollywood, beaches and bikini-clad babes. For a rather impractical man, already given to fantasy, it held out the chance of starting life all over again—the kind of life he really wanted, the one he actually deserved.

And if Ken desperately desired anything, it was a clean slate, a brand-new start. In Rochester, there had been so much disappointment, so many bad memories.

He couldn't catch a break. Life had just dealt him a tough hand. He was angry that his father had died, as if it was a special punishment, a cosmic trap laid just for him. Brenda had stabbed him in the back. Women ... all of them just crapped all over him for no reason.

He used to talk about being dumped on, said an acquaintance in Rochester. Everyone was dumping on him, in his eyes. He never did anything wrong. To him, everything was black and white and everyone was dumping on him, everyone was out to get him...

Chapter 8

In January of 1976, Ken loaded up the Dodge and went for it. He headed south towards Baltimore, hooked up with the Interstate 40 and made the entire trip in a few days. As would become customary with him—maybe he didn't know it yet, but he would be doing plenty of driving over his lifetime—he stopped only briefly along the way, getting snacks out of vending machines and napping in his car.

Once he arrived in sunny California, he was beat; but instead of heading straight to Angelo's in Glendale, he decided to take a spin around downtown Los Angeles. It was the first day of the rest of his life, and he wanted to see what this city had in store for him.

It was the middle of the afternoon when Ken joined the long stream of traffic rolling down Sunset. The sun was still high in the sky, a weekday of all things, and he couldn't believe his eyes.

All his fatigue was forgotten as he took in the view. Girls, hundreds of them, a candy-colored parade in heels and tiny skirts, in bras with no shirts, in hardly anything at all. Black girls, white girls, yellow girls; every kind of girl just there for the taking.

Not that long ago, he had been a married man. He still wanted all that for himself; a wife, kids, the whole cannoli. But now he saw all kinds of strange and wonderful possibilities opening up before him. To his twisted way of thinking he was just a good little Catholic boy from Rochester, and he had never been more aware of it in his life.

This was a whole new world. So big, so bright, so loud.

* * *

Ken started to feel nervous as he made his way to Colorado Street. He hadn't seen Angelo since he was six, when the family had their ill-fated detour to California.

He wasn't sure what to expect; all he could remember about the guy was that he used a lot of foul language. Jenny and Frances weren't happy about it and told Ken not to listen, but Angelo didn't seem to care what they thought either way.

Overall, it was kind of a weird situation, to be driving across the country to move in with a cousin he barely knew. But these were people whose differences and estrangement were easily cancelled out by the Italian creed of La Famiglia. You always lent a hand to those in the clan.

As for Angelo, waiting with little sense of anticipation at the big yellow house on Colorado, he just hoped Ken had grown out of his habit of pissing his pants. He liked to keep his place clean.

When Ken arrived on his doorstep he grunted a lukewarm welcome and gave a perfunctory tour of the house.

Ken was puzzled. Angelo's house had no doors. That meant the spare bedroom, Ken's room, also was doorless, and he would have no privacy. Angelo offered no explanation for the absence of dividers; one could only infer that it was the idiosyncratic preference of a man who chose to know what was happening in any and every room of his house at all times.

There was also no functioning kitchen. Well, there was a space, but no cupboards, pots, pans, working stove. Angelo explained that he always ate out. As it happened the two men dined that evening at the Robin Hood Inn, where Angelo once passed a business card to Cindy Lee Hudspeth, an attractive part-time waitress.

Angelo was hardly talkative. There was no get-to-know-you, no catch up on what each had been up to for the last twenty years. He gave all his attention to his meal, his favorite, fried liver and onions.

Ken felt a little sick watching him cram the oily dreck in his mouth. This was a man of passionate, perverse appetites—maybe more so than his own.

* * *

Once settled in at Colorado Street, Ken quickly realized that life in Los Angeles, at least at first, wasn't quite going to match up to his expectations.

He and Angelo didn't exactly get along. There were profound differences between these two characters.

Angelo was a man who mastered his environment. He was practical, industrious, tidy and temperamentally harsh; he always kept a handle on himself and rarely indulged in loose displays of temper, but he was possessed of a sadistic sense of humor and his actions towards others often seemed motivated by sheer cruelty. Ken found him coarse, and a little frightening.

Kenny had always been prone to idleness and dreaming. Largely passive in the face of life's challenges, he seemed to see himself as a victim much of the time. Angelo thought he was, in short, a sissy and a weakling.

Still, whether it was because Ken wanted Angelo's abrasiveness directed at others rather than himself, or because he secretly coveted the qualities his cousin had that he himself lacked, he quickly fell into a pattern of wanting to please Angelo. Angelo saw that as a useful, if somewhat contemptible quality; he also noted Ken's streak of cunning, and his capacity for silver-tongued charm when in good form.

Despite their differences, the two would also learn that they had something important in common. Neither liked women, but both liked having them around.

Ken was immediately blown away by Angelo's instinctive skill with the ladies.

Despite the fact that Angelo was no oil painting, Colorado Street was often packed with his many female admirers.

Angelo didn't bother to woo or court them, he dispensed with poetry and flowers and got straight to the goods, seemingly by sheer force of some mysterious magnetism. He was brutish, mean and violent, and the girls loved him. Ken decided this Angelo knew something he didn't.

* * *

While not everything was to Ken's liking at Angelo's house, there were certainly opportunities for him to spread his wings. Hollywood was just around the corner, and Angelo was partial to the society of prostitutes.

There were also the female friends and daughters of Angelo's sons. The ethic of La Famiglia was strong: share the bounty. Angelo Anthony Buono III, Angelo's eldest son by Candy, was living in Angelo's den. Peter Buono also visited frequently. Both sons often brought girls to the house, and Angelo and

Ken happily passed them back and forth. Ken also managed to seduce Peter's regular girlfriend, April. This was quite a feather in his cap, but he had to keep quiet about it for obvious reasons.

Angelo's favorite daughter was Grace, who would occasionally spend the night on Angelo's waterbed. Sometimes the whole family would gather in front of the TV and watch pornographic movies together. When the youngsters were present, Angelo would provide a running commentary on what was happening on screen, as if they were watching a soccer match and he was a sports commentator. They needed a real education, something useful.

If all this wasn't wild enough for Ken, there were Angelo's practical jokes and antics with the local hookers. One Sunday evening in February 1976, Angelo, Anthony and Ken were sitting around bored. They decided to hire a call girl from an ad in the *LA Free Press*. After they had all had their turn, Angelo decided they wouldn't pay her. The dumb cunt deserved it for being stupid enough to render her services without demanding up-front payment, he said. Besides, she hadn't been that good anyway.

When the young woman protested, Angelo pulled out a fake police badge, and threatened her with arrest if she didn't scram.

—And that, Angelo said, is how you put a cunt in her place.

Ken was lost in awe and admiration.

* * *

As Ken's stay lengthened, Angelo got testy. Around the house Angelo had taken to calling him Freddy Freeloader, much to the amusement of the others. He started badgering his cousin to get his lazy ass into gear, get a job, and get out of his house.

Ken's first port of call was the Glendale Police Department. He had been rejected by Monroe County; perhaps he would have better luck in LA. As part of his application he was fingerprinted and asked to submit a brief statement about his reasons for wanting to join the department. Ken put his writing skills to good use and prepared a most worthy sounding statement of his suitability for the position, citing his desire to help people, be of service to the community, and contribute to the task of "making America safe". The Glendale PD was initially impressed, but Ken's references from Rochester provoked suspicions, and his application was rejected.

Undeterred, Ken next tried joining the LAPD reserve. He was turned down again, but invited to participate in the citizens ridealong program. Ken was excited about the prospect of learning about inside operations and eagerly signed up, while he continued his employment search elsewhere.

Sighing at the effort, Angelo eventually linked Ken up with his bank manager. She mentioned that her brother worked for the California Land Title Company and that they were looking for new staff.

Ken visited the company that day and, to his surprise, was hired immediately. Initially Ken worked in customer service and records. In his favor, he had no trouble making a good first impression. His neat appearance, politeness and nice-guy demeanor won him that first flush of trust, and after a while he was promoted to Title Officer at the company's head office in Universal City.

With money now flowing, Ken wasted no time in getting out of Angelo's. He was sick of the lack of privacy and had now had his fill of the endless parade of hookers.

He had come to Los Angeles to get on his feet, get himself established, and become a man, and that was what he was going to do. He now had a job; next he set about finding his own apartment and meeting a respectable young woman he could share his life with.

It seems the gods could shine their light even on a wretch like Bianchi, if even only for a while. Much to Ken's surprise, within a couple of months, all his wishes were granted.

* * *

The complex at 809 East Garfield Avenue couldn't have been be more fitting for Ken's new west coast lifestyle. It was a Spanish style block shaped like a horseshoe, the courtyard nestled inside the U and lazily ringed with palm trees.

East Garfield Avenue was just a few blocks from Colorado Street, but now Ken had new female interests to pursue beyond the trash that congregated at Angelo's. A number of young women lived at number 809, among them the pretty but rather reclusive Kristina Weckler.

Ken had tried to engage Kristina several times in hopes of persuading her to go on a date. She was polite, but made it known that his advances were not particularly welcome.

Ken was confused, and more than a little miffed. It wasn't as if she had a boyfriend. She seemed to stay in every night, working on her drawings. The bitch obviously thought she was too good for him.

Ken slunk away and decided to try his luck with another neighbor, Angie Holt, a spunky, fashionable blonde who lived on the opposite side of the court-yard. She was the adventurous type, and was inclined to give the handsome stranger Ken a whirl.

They went out a few times, but Angie's freewheeling California disposition unsettled Ken.

He really had mixed feelings about the women in Los Angeles. Certainly, they were more open to suggestion than the ladies back east. But that was a double-edged sword. It was nice if he could persuade a lady to have a good time; but if she could give herself away so easily, surely she wasn't worth all the dollars he was spending on hamburgers and pop, let alone the type of woman he was looking to settle down with.

He decided he might be wasting his time trying to find a new woman amongst the west coast trollops, and began writing letters to Susan Moore back in Rochester, hoping he could persuade her to reconsider his marriage proposal and join him in Los Angeles.

She had fretted over his impracticality and uncertain future—well now, as he sagely pointed out, those objections were moot: he had a proper job, his own apartment, and even his mother was so impressed with his progress that she had mailed him the down payment for a new car. He used the deposit to acquire a smart blue Cadillac sedan.

Susan agreed to visit Ken in LA, to see for herself how he was coming along. The meeting didn't go well. Ken couldn't help but pry into her dating life back in Rochester, and when he learned that she had been seeing others since he left, he flew into a jealous rage. He kept Susan up until all hours arguing. In the end he told her the whole thing had been a lousy idea and a mistake. She should beat it back east. He never wanted to see her again.

When Susan took Ken at his word and began gathering her things together to leave, he had a change of heart. He burst into tears and begged Susan to stay. He didn't mean it, he said; he'd just lost his temper. Couldn't they forget about it and start over?

Susan found the whole thing ridiculous. She'd forget about it alright—back in Rochester.

She was going to call a cab, but Ken insisted on driving her to the airport. On the way there, he pulled a last ace out of his sleeve and tried to buy himself time by pretending to get lost, so Susan would miss her flight. But Susan was determined to get the hell out of LA and away from Ken; after they finally arrived at the airport, she simply waited for the next flight out.

* * *

With his plan to win Susan back a failure, Ken quickly resumed his relationship with Angie Holt. But she too soon grew weary of Ken's jealous and controlling ways, and without his knowledge, was gradually trading him in for more laid-back company.

When Ken learned there was some bowl-smoking surfer dude living in Angie's apartment, he was outraged. He stalked Angie down to the communal laundry one evening and cornered her in there. He unleashed a barrage of invective on her and got in her face, waving his finger. She was no good. She was nothing but a two-timing whore.

Angie stood her ground; she told Ken to grow up, shoved him out of the way with her basket, and got out of there.

A couple of weeks later, Angie and her date returned to her apartment to find the place a mess, the TV missing and a big hole in Angie's diaphragm, apparently punched with a pen.

Chapter 9

If Kelli Boyd had any idea Ken Bianchi was capable of such things, she wouldn't have given him the time of day. But whenever the classy blonde secretary at Cal-Land was within radar, Ken was on his best behavior; all "have a nice day" with his suit and tie and perfectly groomed hair.

Kelli had taken his fancy, but from a distance. He wasn't yet assured of an in, but when he got talking to Kelli's sister Linda, who also worked at the Universal City office, he saw his opportunity. Kelli's sister was having trouble with her car.

Ken swooped in, full of manly gallantry and mechanical know-how, and got Linda's car running again. Linda was due to head out of town on a trip, so she was grateful for Ken's help. She offered Ken some money by way of thanks.

Don't worry about it, Ken said with a wave of his hand; helping was its own reward as far as he was concerned.

A short time later at the office, Kelli and Linda were talking when Ken walked by and smiled.

—Who's that hunk? Kelli said to Linda.

—Oh, that's Ken, said Linda. Ken Bianchi. He's new. He's a real nice guy.

* * *

Like Ken, Kelli Boyd wasn't a Los Angeles native. Like Ken, she felt a little out of place there.

She had grown up in Bellingham, a sleepy coastal town just south of the Canadian border. She was grateful for the job opportunities in Los Angeles, but California life wasn't really for her. She wanted to settle down with someone, and it was hard to meet men who were serious about commitment.

Kelli had spoken to Ken a few times at the office, and, based on his appearance at least, she liked him already. He was neat, respectful, well put together; the classic tall, dark and handsome man of every woman's dreams. Still, the two were a little shy around each other, and she hadn't really got well acquainted with him.

That was about to change. Some of Kelli's colleagues invited Ken to a party to which she was also going.

It was a typical Los Angeles young people's gathering, the booze and marijuana flowing freely to disco music. Kelli closely observed how Ken carried himself. He interacted with the others but only took a couple of drinks and didn't partake of the scoob that was being passed around. She was impressed, gathering the impression of a serious young man, someone who might someday make a good husband and father. To Kelli, Ken was not only physically attractive but seemed decent—not an easy combination to find in Los Angeles.

When the two finally got to talking, Ken didn't leer down her blouse but instead shared with her his dream of a home and family.

—I lost my Dad when I was young, you know, he said. I just want to give someone the things I never had.

Kelli's heart swelled with empathy for her handsome and sensitive coworker. She knew what it was like to come from a broken home. Her own parents had divorced when she was thirteen.

The two would learn they had more in common. Both had married early into relationships that had foundered rapidly and painfully, and neither had since been able to find partners they felt they could settle down with. They talked deep into the night, sharing their hopes and fears. As the hours passed they realized they had long neglected talk with the other partygoers; they were only interested in each other.

After the party, Ken escorted Kelli home. There was an awkward moment at the door. Would they say goodbye, or would the night "go on"? Kelli made an impulse decision and invited Ken inside, and not too long after, the inevitable happened.

This decision led to another awkward moment the next morning. Putting out on the first date wasn't customary for Kelli, but she really liked Ken, and things had "just happened". She suddenly felt shy, and a little ashamed. When Ken left that morning she wasn't sure she was going to hear from him again. And she worried about the potential fallout of her actions at the office.

Neither had one another's measure. As for Ken, giving a second chance to an easy girl wasn't usual for him either. But he broke his own rules and called Kelli a few days later. The period of uncertainty passed, and the two quickly fell into an apparently normal relationship; surely a testament to the mystery of human attraction.

So sure were they of their feelings that within weeks, Kelli had moved into Ken's apartment. The lovers settled into a routine of days at the office followed by quiet evenings at home, as if they were already a married couple.

Kelli preferred reading to television, but sometimes she would sit with Ken and watch his favorite shows. Given his passion for policing, it wasn't surprising that Ken's preferred programs were cop dramas. But Kelli learned that Ken could be very sentimental. The other kind of shows he liked were comedy-dramas celebrating family life, such as *Eight Is Enough*, a series centered on a whitebread Sacramento family with eight children. To Kelli, Ken was clearly longing for some sense of belonging he missed out on. She quietly hoped that they might be going to create that kind of happiness together.

Kelli probably thought they had plenty of time to turn their dreams into reality. As it happened, by May 1977, she was already pregnant. The circumstances, however, were far from ideal.

* * *

Ken's possessive nature emerged fairly early in their relationship. When Kelli told him she wanted to go on a road trip with a girlfriend from Bellingham, Ken immediately objected. It wasn't safe, he said. Two women driving around alone in the wilds—there could be anyone or anything out there, waiting to pounce.

Kelli dug her heels in, demonstrating a degree of stubbornness Ken was unused to. He had already made so many exceptions for this woman. He let her go, quietly stewing in his rancor.

After the girlfriend travelled south to meet with Kelli the two drove east as far as Denver. There they decided to spend a night at the Ramada Inn, and, tired from the day's journey, headed to the hotel bar to unwind.

Sadly for Kelli, Ken's premonitions were correct. A couple of gentlemen at the bar decided the two attractive young ladies had no business socializing there by themselves. Loathe to be difficult, Kelli and her friend tolerated the men's company while enjoying the drinks and music.

One of the men invited Kelli's friend to visit the bar with him, leaving Kelli alone at the table with the other. Watching her companion without distractions, Kelli now realized the man was drunk. Glassy eyed, he sagged against the table. He told Kelli he was about to pass out. He needed to get back to his room, and he wasn't sure he could make it there by himself.

Kelli was reluctant, but the man had bought her some drinks, and in his stupor he seemed harmless enough. As they made their way to his room, Kelli supporting him on her arm, she became aware of the man's bulk. Tall and powerfully built, he hung on her shoulder like a lump, pouring his booze-soaked breath all over her. He had clearly been drinking for many hours.

When they arrived at his room, the man's mood suddenly flipped. The stupor evaporated—he wasn't drunk at all. He grabbed Kelli by the arm and shoved her inside. She struggled against him, guessing what was coming next, but it was futile. The man made it clear he was going to get what he wanted, or beat her senseless. Either way they were going to have some fun.

* * *

Shaken and degraded, Kelli returned to Los Angeles. The trauma was compounded by shame. Ken had warned her what could happen, but she had been so headstrong. Now that he had been proven right, she was too embarrassed to tell him what happened. She decided to put the whole thing behind her, and try to forget it ever happened. She never reported the rape or told a soul, Ken included.

Kelli's reaction was typical of many rape victims. She feared that by sharing her ordeal, it would make it more real. Confessing might also invite disbelief and accusation, which would be intolerable on top of the agony she had already endured. Burying the rape in the deep recesses of her mind seemed the best option. Maybe she could just wake up to a new day, as if it had all been a bad dream.

But that wasn't to be. In the weeks that followed an ugly reminder of the assault appeared in the shape of strange symptoms. Kelli had contracted a venereal disease from the man who raped her.

What was worse, she had passed the infection to Ken. She now had no choice but to confess everything. It would be far worse if he thought she had cheated on him.

Kelli steeled herself for Ken's reaction but hoped for the best. She knew Ken was jealous, but she had never lied to him before. He was a caring, protective lover; she had been through a terrible ordeal. He would understand. He would comfort her, and together they would sort it out.

Ken's reaction wasn't exactly what Kelli wished for. But she probably didn't know him well enough to realize that, from his perspective, it was generous. He didn't quite fly off the handle. But he was suspicious. If she had been raped, where was the police report? Why hadn't she called them and pressed charges?

Perhaps, if Kelli had really known Ken, she might have been even more bothered by his subdued response. Because Ken was quietly going crazy, his paranoia and rage snowballing under cover of a superficially supportive exterior. The only reason he was holding it together was because the relationship was new, and no matter what, he didn't want to lose Kelli.

The couple went to a doctor to be treated for the infection. There, they were presented with another shock: Kelli was expecting. At first Ken was reeling at the possibility that the child in Kelli's womb was another man's. But the doctor told them that Kelli was too far along; the child had been conceived well before the trip to Denver.

Ken was overjoyed. He forgot all about the STD and the possibility of Kelli's cheating. He was going to be a father. His dreams of a family of his own were about to come true.

Chapter 10

Kelli shared Ken's excitement, but her feelings were more mixed. Cracks were appearing in the relationship. A baby was a chance for a new start, maybe an opportunity for Ken to prove his maturity, but it also tethered her to a man she was beginning to wonder was any kind of realistic prospect for a long-term partner.

The couple had recently moved to a new apartment in the Tamarind complex at Franklin Avenue in Hollywood. Kelli allowed herself to hope that the move heralded better things for the relationship. The new apartment was larger and in better condition than the cramped flat they had shared at East Garfield. But after an initial burst of optimism, Kelli found her hopes fading.

There was the matter of Ken's jealousy. Ken demanded Kelli's undivided attention, and when she wasn't at work, he expected her to stay home. She had cajoled and pleaded with him to be allowed to go on the road trip. That had turned out badly, so now he had even more reason to doubt her. He resented the other people in her life, especially any men. He was morbidly preoccupied with her interactions with male colleagues, and even seemed to rankle at time she spent with her brothers.

Another source of tension was Angelo.

While on the surface Ken had eagerly embraced his new identity of upstanding family man and corporate drone, he hadn't really made a break from Angelo and the sordid delights of Colorado Street. Now, it was really a matter of enjoying the best of both worlds, collecting all the benefits of a respectable image while still enjoying the odd slice of cake.

While Ken didn't like Kelli being away from home, he never denied himself the freedoms he refused to extend to her, and when he tired of watching television, he would head over to Angelo's to "play cards".

Kelli didn't care for Angelo, and the antipathy was mutual. Angelo gave Kelli the creeps. The things that came out of his mouth, and just the way he handled himself, left her profoundly uneasy. It was obvious he held women in no regard at all, even his own mother, who Kelli had heard Angelo refer to as "the old cunt" on more than one occasion.

Such disrespect was anathema to Kelli's family values, and she didn't understand or appreciate it one bit. She also wondered what it said about Ken that he maintained a friendship with such a person. But she did understand that Angelo was family to Ken, and things worked a bit differently in their Italian culture. Gross defects of character could be overlooked in the scheme of family loyalty. And she grasped that Ken, new to the city and with few friends, needed something to do outside work and home.

Sometimes Ken would stay at Angelo's until the early hours of the morning. Angelo didn't drink at all, and Ken drank little; Kelli wondered how simple card games could be keeping them entertained so long. Ken's lengthy absences bothered her, but it was easy to dismiss them as a product of Angelo's bad influence.

But then, things took a turn for the worse. Ken started "chucking sickies", calling into work with flu or headache and then heading over to Angelo's. Kelli knew Ken's job could be dull at times, but he needed to hold onto it, particularly with their existing financial worries and now, a baby on the way. The couple held a joint account for their mutual expenses, but Kelli always seemed to be contributing the lion's share of the cash. Ken was financially irresponsible and forever seemed to be spending money he didn't have. Kelli resented Ken's recklessness with money and his tendency to not uphold his commitments. She certainly wondered if he was mature enough to be a father.

* * *

Kelli's worries about their money problems soon came to a head. One day Ken's superiors at Cal-Land opened his desk drawer and found a bag of marijuana stashed inside. He was fired immediately.

Kelli was aghast at Ken's irresponsible attitude. Someone must have planted the marijuana, Ken said—she knew he didn't smoke pot!

Perhaps she could accept that, although the story sounded doubtful. Either way, the takeaway from all of this was that now—with a baby on the way—they were dependent on her income alone.

Kelli was tearing her hair out, and nobody would have blamed her if at this point, she fled from Ken and never looked back. But despite the difficulties of their union, Kelli loved him. At his best, he was the most tender, gentle and romantic of men. The lows of their relationship were always followed by highs that, for her, ultimately balanced out. The good times were the best she'd ever had.

When tensions mounted, Kelli would sometimes leave the apartment to spend a day or two with friends or her brothers. This was the first sign of the familiar rollercoaster of an on-off relationship, breaking apart and coming together again many times over. For now, however, it just seemed that taking a momentary cool off was a very adult solution to niggling problems.

Kelli would return to Tamarind to find the hood of her car festooned with flowers, and thoughtfully crafted love poems tucked in behind the windscreen wipers.

Kelli dismissed Ken's jealousy and much of his erratic behavior as a product of his great love for her and his insecurities. Despite his looks Ken seemed to worry deep down that he didn't have what it took to hold onto her. Some other man with more to offer might at any moment steal her away.

As for his irresponsibility, and now joblessness, she knew Ken was a bit of a dreamer. It was frustrating, but that side of him could be very sweet too.

There was something very childlike and vulnerable about Ken. At twenty-six he still loved kid's cartoons. Kelli had gone to the cinema with him to see the Disney film *Pete the Dragon*. She wasn't much interested in children's animation, but happily indulged Ken's own youthful enthusiasm.

Ken was also a lover of comics. His favorite was *Prince Valiant*, a courtly medieval epic concerning the heroic exploits of the main character and his knights of Camelot. That was appropriate; in his dreams, Ken was the honourable knight defending the damsel in distress. But Ken seemed to not care much for reality, where everyday life made its mundane demands, where hard work was the price paid for incremental progress, and not all ladies were delicate, virtuous damsels.

Kelli's instincts towards Ken were almost motherly. She hoped to take him under her wing and gently steer him in the right direction. She rebuffed his repeated proposals of marriage, trying to make him realize that only by displaying greater maturity and stability could he hope to convince her to take his hand.

* * *

Kelli was always hoping that things would turn around. She was encouraged when Ken secured a new job at Stewart West Coast Title, similar to his previous position at Cal-Land. She quietly prayed that he wouldn't screw this one up.

He had also come up with another scheme to help ease their money worries. As far as Kelli knew, Ken had earned his accreditations in psychology well before they met. She had seen the framed certificates, but she was nonetheless skeptical of his plan to set up a discount counseling service.

Ken in fact managed to convince a proper psychologist who operated from offices on Lankershim of his bona fides, and was offered a suite from which to run his business in the same block. Ken knew Californians responded to window dressing, so he decked out the office with psychology titles to make it look legitimate. He printed and distributed flyers, and dutifully went to his office and waited for his phone to ring, but he got very few calls, and failed to build a clientele.

Yes, she loved him, and there were two more compelling reasons she stayed by his side. One was the baby. Another was that Ken himself was in a frail condition. He might even die, he told her.

A couple months previous, Ken had developed a persistent cough and occasional breathing difficulties. Kelli had recently adopted two kittens, and Ken did have a history of allergies and asthma, so he put his symptoms down to that, but decided to go to a doctor to get checked out anyway.

Upon returning from the clinic, Ken was unusually quiet. After a while Kelli was able to pry the bad news out of him. The doctors had given him a chest X-ray, and something unusual, a mass, had been detected. They wanted to take a biopsy to be sure of what they were dealing with.

Kelli was worried out of her mind. She took the day off work so she could drive Ken to the hospital on the day of the procedure, but he strangely insisted on going alone. As the day wore on with no sign of Ken, Kelli's worry grew into panic. It was well after dinner time and there was no sign of him. Finally, at around eight, he arrived home with the excuse that he had left the hospital and gone to play cards at Angelo's.

Kelli was puzzled. There she was worried sick, and he was playing cards?

She melted when, with a hangdog expression, he told her that he had gone to Angelo's because he couldn't face telling her what had happened. The tumor was malignant. He had cancer.

Kelli felt like her whole world was collapsing. Would the baby have to grow up without a father? She tried to hold back her tears, to be strong for Ken, but every now and then they spilled out of her as the apparent hopelessness of their situation overwhelmed her.

Ken, on the other hand, was calm and stoic. He seemed resigned to the situation. He had to be strong for Kelli, who was not only struggling with the effects of pregnancy, but was now facing the prospect of raising a child alone.

He comforted her and did his best to reassure her that everything would be okay. He'd need radiation treatments, he explained to her solemnly. Possibly chemotherapy as well. But it wasn't a big deal. He could go into the hospital as an outpatient. Life would go on as usual. The treatments would wear him down and make him feel a little sick, so of course he would have to take some time off work. But the disruption to their lives would be minimal. They'd get through it. He could either attend his treatments alone, or she could drive him to the hospital and wait in the car while he met with the doctors. Either way it was completely unnecessary for her to be exposed to any of the unpleasantness going on in the clinic.

Kelli was perplexed. How could Ken be making so light of this? He seemed almost embarrassed about the diagnosis, as if it was a moral failing. He wanted Kelli bothered by his illness as little as possible. Her heart went out to him; obviously it made him feel less of a man. He was supposed to be her support and protector, and now, when Kelli herself was so vulnerable, it was as if their roles were reversed.

Kelli was hurt by the way Ken was locking her out in his time of need. On the first scheduled day of treatment she drove him to the hospital and waited nervously in the parking lot, ruminating over the uncertain future. Would Ken recover? How were the treatments going to affect him?

As time wore on, Kelli's loneliness turned to confusion. Ken continued with his treatments but there seemed no change in his condition. He still coughed and complained of weakness, but otherwise, he seemed no different than before. Stony-faced and button lipped, he seemed to continue through life robotically, refusing to share his struggles with her.

He needed many days off work, and spent more and more time slouching around at the apartment. Despite his weakness, he wasn't too sick to spend time with Angelo, and continued to disappear to Colorado Street intermittently.

Kelli was worried about Ken, but she was worried about their financial situation, too. Without any sense of how Ken's illness was progressing, she asked him if she could speak to his doctor. He reacted angrily, insisting she drop it. It seemed Ken was so troubled, he refused to even talk about it.

Ken and Kelli had many fights about money, about his cancer, about his inconsiderate habits. Sometimes Ken would borrow Kelli's car and fail to re-fill the gas tank. She would get up in the morning for work and find her car wouldn't start. When Kelli tried to raise any issues in the relationship, she was made aware of Ken's ugly temper. He would get in her face, yell and wave his finger at her before storming off somewhere, usually to Angelo's. Nothing ever got resolved, and Kelli began to feel that she didn't matter.

The happy times between fights were shorter, and further apart. By December Kelli was in the third trimester of her pregnancy, and between that and all the arguments, her normal condition was one of tension and grumpiness.

Ken used Kelli's foul mood as an excuse to spend even more time at Angelo's.

For Kelli's part, she found Ken's moods intolerably volatile. One day he was sweet and gentle, another he was angry for no apparent reason, and would rage at her, spewing out insults and foul language. Sometimes he lapsed into icy silences lasting hours or days. He could be passive, timid, almost babyish, crying out for her love and attention; and then, at the drop of the hat, go on the attack. The change was like night and day, and Kelli got tired of never knowing what state he would be in when he walked in the door, or she returned home.

Eventually the fights turned physical. On one occasion, when Ken was bellowing and wagging his finger at her, the pressure became too much and Kelli snapped, striking Ken. She didn't appreciate being yelled at just because Ken didn't want to deal with their issues, particularly when she was already feeling so bad.

Enraged, Ken struck Kelli with a blow that sent her crashing against the wall and onto the floor. Stunned, Kelli instinctively drew her arm across her stomach.

Ken broke down in a gale of tears, horrified at his own actions. My God, he said, I could have killed my own child!

He was so, so very sorry and ashamed. He made sure Kelli was okay. It would never, ever happen again—he swore on his life.

But it was too late. Kelli drew a line. Violence was something she could not tolerate, and once was good enough for her. She announced she was moving out—this time for good.

* * *

Kelli had more than one reason to flee. She didn't care at all for life at the Tamarind Apartments, even if the place was larger and a little nicer than East Garfield. The block was closer to the Hollywood riff-raff, and most of the residents were half crazy. There had been a few long and worrisome nights, with all manner of shouting, banging and carrying on.

Everyone had heard about the Hillside Strangler, and Kelli, like every woman in Los Angeles, was terrified. She, along with her female colleagues, had gotten into the habit of carrying around a whistle. Some of the girls she worked with were even carrying weapons.

One night there was screaming and scuffling on the ground floor. In the days to come Kelli was horrified when she learned that the Hillside Strangler had abducted one of the victims, a young prostitute, from the very block in which she lived.

That was just too much. She wanted to get far away from the place. What if the strangler was living right there in the complex? Either way, he had some connection to the place, and she didn't want to hang around to find out if he was coming back.

Even stranger, the police had come to the apartment to talk to Ken. Of course he'd done his best to help, but he knew as little as the other residents. Ken, like everyone else in Los Angeles, had been following the case in the newspapers and on TV. Here and there he would share his insights with Kelli. He was curious about the developments, and given his background and interest in policing, that didn't surprise her at all.

In December Ken took part in the ridealong program with the LAPD. Being the friendly guy he was, Ken chatted amiably with the officers about current affairs, and the Hillside Strangler was one topic of conversation he was particularly interested in. The cops, of course, couldn't offer Ken any enlightenment beyond what details he would have already gleaned from the media. Ken asked for an unofficial tour of the sites where bodies had been found, which they politely refused.

—Hey Ken, Kelli said after the police left after the Martin murder investigation. You sure you're not the strangler?

They both laughed.

Chapter 11

As 1977 drew to a close, there was little Christmas cheer in Ken and Kelli's world.

They were drifting further and further apart, emotionally and physically. Kelli spent days at a time with friends and relatives. Eventually she moved in on a more permanent basis with her brother Gerald.

Ken and Kelli kept breaking up and getting back together. But finally, they weren't together in any meaningful sense at all.

Cementing Kelli's decision to distance herself, Ken got fired yet again, this time for taking too much time off work without valid medical certificates. Stewart West Coast Title were suspicious about Ken's story of having lung cancer. Ken of course gave Kelli a different story about the reason for his dismissal.

Ken found a casual replacement position at a nursing home, a considerable demotion in both salary and dignity, and with his financial situation in tatters, had to give up the apartment at Tamarind and move into a share house with some friends of Kelli's brothers.

Kelli had not entirely given up on Ken, because she invited him for a short break to Bellingham to stay with her family. Ken took this as a sign that Kelli was still invested in their future, but upon their return to Los Angeles, Kelli refused Ken's suggestion to move back in together, let alone consider marriage, even if she was carrying his child.

In January 1978, Kelli quit her job at Cal-Land in preparation for the baby, due in February. Despite all their problems, Ken and Kelli were thrilled about the "little person", as Ken was fond of calling it.

It so happened that Ken came to parenthood at the time that trendy new concepts of involved fathering were sprouting in pockets of California. Home birthing and Lamaze training was all the rage. The ebullient father-to-be was one hundred percent on board and joined Kelli in Lamaze classes; the couple were hoping to deliver the baby at home, and Ken would be fully involved in the process at each step. The training and their excitement about the birth brought them together, and Kelli felt a tentative renewal of their bond.

All didn't work out according to plan, however. In the week leading up to her due date, Kelli began to go into a protracted "false" labor. All signs were there that the child was coming, but nothing happened except unproductive cramping. Kelli was in a great deal of pain, and began to panic, sure that something was wrong.

When her waters finally broke, Kelli was rushed to hospital where the doctors discovered the baby was trapped in the birth canal. Ken had to wait anxiously outside the delivery room while the doctors struggled with a medical emergency. Ken could not be with Kelli at the crucial hour, and all the training had been for nothing.

Ryan came into the world on 23 February 1978. His name was chosen from Kelli's favorite daytime soap, *Ryan's Hope*. A more cynical view is that it had something to do with the fake name Bianchi had used when he lured prostitute Kimberly Martin, victim number seven, to her death. The little boy bore a notable resemblance to his father in baby photos kept by Frances.

Ken was overjoyed that Kelli had given him a son. Of course, he told her that he would be happy either way; a girl would have been just as welcome. But privately he was relieved and delighted that God in his wisdom had not sent him such a lesser being. Here instead was a project that could legitimately command his interest.

After seeing Kelli in the delivery room, Ken immediately called his mother back east, who shared in his rapture. Frances told Ken that she knew he would make a wonderful father.

As it turned out, on his good days Ken was the very model of progressive social ideals, enthusiastically changing diapers and coordinating the bath time ritual. As long as he was physically present, Kelli could count on him for any assistance with Ryan's care. But that was just the problem; Ken often wasn't present, and when he was, Kelli often wished he'd take a hike.

In the afterglow of Ryan's birth, Kelli had begun to contemplate trying over with Ken. Instead, just a month later, the relationship was tanking again. Despite the fact that Ken, in Kelli's eyes, was a loving father, he would never make a good partner. The patterns of laziness and irresponsibility continued. He was forever goofing off with Angelo. Ken's Cadillac was repossessed when he failed to make the repayments on his loan. Kelli knew Ken was short of money, but Ken had simply ignored the bills and evaded the creditors until they hunted him down and took the car away.

Ken's housemates at Corona Drive were also unhappy with him and finally kicked him out. He was only supposed to stay a short time, but had well and truly outworn his welcome by borrowing their cars without permission and skipping on rent.

There was something else the Corona Drive residents were concerned about. In amongst Ken's possessions they had spotted a police badge. Everyone knew the Hillside Strangler was, or posed as, a police officer. They didn't really believe Ken could be the strangler, but they knew he was no cop and he had no business carrying a badge. It bothered them enough that they mentioned it to a neighbor who happened to be an officer of the Glendale PD.

* * *

Kelli Boyd, having resigned her job, now had nothing tying her to Los Angeles apart from Ken. She was homesick for the tranquility of Washington. She missed the normality and stability that her family provided, and she wanted her parents to have a closer relationship with their grandchild. She told Ken she was thinking of taking Ryan back to Bellingham, so he could grow up in a more wholesome environment.

At first Ken thought Kelli was proposing that they relocate together with the baby. But when he started asking about the details of the plan, Kelli expressed significant reservations about Ken joining the party.

This talk of a more permanent separation, and the possibility that Ryan could be taken away from him, made Ken nervous; but he was optimistic that it was only talk. Deep down Kelli loved him, and she would reconsider when she saw Ken getting back on his feet.

To this end, ever-resourceful Ken quickly landed a new, significantly more prestigious job. He applied for an orderly role at Verdugo Hills Hospital, supporting his submission with his medical experience as an ambulance attendant in Rochester. The HR department at Verdugo Hills were also delighted to see this candidate held an accreditation in psychology from Columbia University, and work experience at the Strong Memorial Hospital. Wooed by such impressive credentials, they offered Ken a more senior position than the one he had applied for, sterilizing and delivering surgical equipment.

Once again financially solvent, Ken moved into a new apartment on Verdugo Road, one that he hoped could entice Kelli back to him since he could now offer a more suitable environment to raise a child. Combining his first wages with a loan from an old girlfriend Sheryl Kellison, with whom he had renewed his liaison since being on the outs with Kelli, he also bought a cheap new car.

But Ken had miscalculated Kelli's willingness to overlook the long history of troubles over a few short-term gains. Kelli had been around the block with Ken enough to know that any improvement in his fortunes tended to be short-lived. Besides, it wasn't even just about what he could provide materially for her and the baby. Ken's inability to hold down a job or a residence spoke to deeper defects of character, as did his lies and his outbursts. Ken never told her why he really lost his job at Stewart West Coast Title, but she had a hinky feeling about the cancer diagnosis and wondered about the psychology diplomas. When Ken told her the boy needed a father, she agreed; but she wasn't at all sure that Ken was the kind of father Ryan needed.

Kelli was still young and attractive, and even as a single mother, she knew she had a lot to offer the right guy. It wasn't unreasonable to think that she could meet someone else, someone who could offer what Ken had so fervently promised but failed to deliver. By March, she had made her mind up: she was taking Ryan and moving back to Bellingham, and they would be going alone. Ryan had only been in the world a few short weeks when Kelli packed up their belongings in her car and began driving north. Kelli's plan was to stay temporarily with her father and stepmother until her application for welfare was approved. She and Ryan would then find a place on their own.

When Kelli left him, taking his child with her, Ken was overwhelmed by ancient and painful feelings of abandonment. It seemed he hadn't left his pattern of getting dumped on back in Rochester. He probably didn't have enough insight to realize that no matter where he ran to, he had to take himself along for the ride.

Ken wallowed in bitterness and this dark resurrection of the memories of all who had forsaken and betrayed him in the past. It seemed that he was forever destined to be alone, no matter what he did, how he tried, how much he loved.

Those he loved most always left: his father left him, Brenda had abandoned him, and now Kelli was gone, taking Ryan, a piece of Ken himself.

It seemed the deepest, most final cut.

Chapter 12

It could be said in Los Angeles through 1977 and early 1978, Kenneth Bianchi had been living two lives, one with Kelli Boyd and another with Angelo Buono. Kelli was the woman he had fallen in love with, the mother of his child. Angelo, his cousin, had been almost a stranger, but in a short space of time, had become so much more.

It wasn't so much that the two were particularly close, or even got along well. There were many arguments and temporary falling outs. The mercurial Ken drove Angelo up the wall with his pie-in-the-sky schemes, his laziness and his sloppy judgment. Honestly, the guy was a sandwich short of a picnic. Ironically, Angelo told Grace and his son's girlfriends to stay away from Ken. He was "crazy" and bad news.

As for Ken, he was frightened of Angelo's temper, his icy vindictiveness, his pure power. He never wanted any of that pointed at him. Better to help the guy out; lend a hand. And so it was; whatever their differences, they were bonded by shared interests that were beyond the pale of the normies, and created, of their own mysterious magic, a positively intimate little world.

Ken was always whining about his money hassles. Angelo thought he was nothing but a bum, but at that time, with Ken living rent-free in his spare bedroom, he had motivation beyond familial concern to help Ken find cash.

Angelo came up with an idea. Maybe the two of them could set up a part-time pimping racket. There were always girls around willing to open their legs; why not put them to work? Angelo had a potential client base right at his fingertips through his car upholstery business.

Ken was a little soft, but with his good looks and his chivalrous nice-guy routines he could put women at ease, particularly the kinds of women who might be intimidated by Angelo's more unpolished brand of appeal. Angelo knew plenty of whores already, but it was no good ripping off another guy's merchandise—they needed to find fresh meat. Angelo tasked Ken with recruitment; he himself would manage operations.

The party at which Ken first met Kelli Boyd had been hosted by a mutual colleague at Cal-Land, Mary Forsberg. Mary was a party girl, fond of a drink and a joint. There were other parties on that winter when Ken and Kelli had begun dating, and at one of these, Ken was present but Kelli was not.

Sabra Hannan was sixteen, and hardly wise to the ways of Los Angeles. A runaway and aspiring model from Phoenix, Arizona, she had so far picked up only one gig, and was hunting the big time in California.

When Ken laid eyes on Sabra at the party, he liked what he saw. Petite but busty, her flawless face framed by a cloud of blonde hair, she closely resembled a doll. Exactly what they were after.

Ken introduced himself and set about loosening Sabra up with a few drinks. When he learned she was looking for modeling work, he told her he had plenty of contacts in the industry.

—What experience do you have? Ken asked pompously, enjoying the fleeting feeling of status conferred by his new role.

—Well, said Sabra, not much. I done some work for Evinrude a while back. The jobs were hard to come by back home.

Evinrude was an outboard motor manufacturer. Ken was picturing Sabra in a bikini on some boat, slathered in suntan oil. Nice.

—You've been running with a dud crowd. You're so gorgeous you should be making hundreds of dollars a week!

Ken promised he could make it happen for her just by snapping his fingers. It was a whole different ballgame in LA; she needed to link up with someone like him, who knew the city and could get her the good jobs.

Sabra hummed and hawed. This Ken seemed like a nice guy and he seemed to know what he was talking about, but she didn't know him, and she had to head back to Phoenix for a while to visit friends. She took Ken's number and said she would call if she changed her mind.

Ken left the party that night unsure if he would ever hear from Sabra again. But hey, he was practicing his game, and if Sabra fell through, there would be others.

Still, Sabra was really something. He sure hoped she would get in touch.

Luckily for Ken, and unluckily for Sabra, after visiting with friends in Lubbock, Texas, and heading onto Phoenix, Sabra ran out of cash. She called Ken and said she was ready to head to LA and work, but she had no money for a ticket.

—Don't worry about a thing, Ken said, I'll take care of that. I can even offer you a place to stay until you get on your feet. No charge.

The free board was at Angelo's, where Sabra would end up staying much longer than she anticipated.

Ken reported the good news back to Angelo. There was a hitch though; Sabra thought she would be doing modeling jobs, not whoring. No problem, said Angelo. He was very confident they would be able to warm Sabra up, or wear her down. Whatever worked.

She wouldn't have much option either way; they were paying her fare to Los Angeles, so she would already be in their debt.

Sabra Hannan had just been lured into the game by one of the oldest cons in the book. In Los Angeles, pimps regularly pose as entertainment and modeling scouts to snare naïve and hopeful runaways. Hollywood's "casting couch", a place where modeling jobs and film roles are exchanged for sexual favors, had always blurred the distinction between a prostitute and an entertainer in Los Angeles. For Sabra, however, there would be no payment in fame and honors—she was going to have to give it away for free. She just didn't know it yet.

Instead, when Sabra stepped off the plane, she was excited about the future. She was about to embark on a whole new life, with stacks of money, cool new friends and fun stories to tell back home.

Ken was waiting for her at the gate. When she saw the Cadillac, she was impressed. The guy obviously had money.

On the drive back, Ken talked a lot, mostly about himself. It sounded like this guy knew everyone in Los Angeles. He told her if she just gave things a little time and put in the hard work, she could make it really big. Just wait and see, he said. In the city of dreams magic happens every day.

Angelo had given Ken instructions to take Sabra to The Sands, where she would stay for one night. The idea was to really warm Sabra up to the possibilities, to get her thinking she would be well rewarded ... if she behaved. Then, later, she would be much more malleable.

Ken booked her in at the hotel under his own name, "Kenneth A. Bianchi, PhD". Before he left for the night, he showed her some purloined diamonds and promised her one as a bonus after her first week's work. Sabra went to bed deliriously happy and excited.

The next day, Ken picked her up and took her back to Colorado Street to meet Angelo, one of his "contacts in the business". Sabra looked a little crest-fallen at the downgrading of her accommodations, so Angelo kept the ruse going by taking out a wad of bills and peeling off a hundred so Sabra could buy some new clothes.

Ken was the kind, polite one; Angelo was a little rough around the edges. But really, both men seemed very pleasant and helpful. Angelo told Sabra she could sleep in the spare room free of charge.

The only condition of her staying was that she wasn't to go anywhere with-out telling him first. Ken was talking to the clients and it was important that Sabra be available at a moment's notice should an opening arise.

* * *

Days passed, and there were no modeling jobs for Sabra. Things might be a little slow for a while, Ken explained; in July many people were out of town for holidays.

Sabra was bored. There was nothing going on at Angelo's—if you didn't count the parade of strange, sometimes scary, people wandering in and out of the place at all hours—and she couldn't leave. She started to wonder if coming to Los Angeles had been a mistake.

Then one afternoon Ken excitedly told her that a job had come though. It wasn't quite what Sabra was used to, although Ken promised it would pay well. An artist was looking for nudes for life drawing. He would need to see some shots first to see that Sabra had the right look for what he had in mind. Sabra bought the story. She took her clothes off and Angelo took several snaps of her on his waterbed. But not long after, Ken had bad news for Sabra. The client had pulled out. She wasn't what they were after; a little on the large side.

Sabra was pretty put out by the insinuation she was fat. Standards must be different here in Los Angeles? Mostly she was worried about money. She owed these guys, there were no jobs, and she couldn't leave.

Angelo said he had an idea of how she could make some cash in the mean-time. Had she ever considered prostitution?

Sabra was insulted. No, she would never even entertain the possibility and if she had known those would be the kinds of jobs she would be doing, she never would have signed up.

Angelo was disgusted by Sabra's insubordination. Obviously this white trash from Phoenix thought she was really something. Inside he seethed, but this was no time to make a scene. He left Sabra alone to rethink her situation.

Don't worry, she'll break soon, he said to Ken.

Sabra still had the hundred bucks from Angelo. A week had passed, there were no gigs and she hadn't earned a cent. Disillusioned and dirty at her captors, she decided to get what Angelo had promised her, some new clothes. Without telling him, she walked out the door and headed down Colorado Street on foot towards Eagle Rock Plaza.

A couple hours later Sabra returned, having spent most of the hundred. What was about to happen next would make her wish she had held onto the money and kept it moving to the bus station.

As Sabra approached the house she saw Angelo standing in the entryway with his arms crossed, like some angry dad whose daughter was home late from the prom.

Sabra's first instinct was to make a run for it. But it was too late. He had already seen her. She tried walking up to the house with an air of sass, like nothing was wrong.

Angelo grabbed Sabra by the arm.

—Hey! What did I say about leaving the house, huh? What did I say?

—You said ... you said ... Sabra trembled and stuttered. Don't go out without telling me...

—That's right! And what did you do?! Huh? What did you do? You do that, that one thing, that one very thing I told you not to do!

Angelo had Sabra by the shoulders, shaking her. Ken stood a few feet away, thumbs in pockets, glowering. Long gone was the friendly guy who'd give you the shirt off his back.

—Don't you get it bitch? Angelo ranted. You living in my house, you live under my rules. Get in there!

Angelo pushed Sabra down the hallway and into the spare room.

—Kenny! Get the towel.

Ken disappeared to the bathroom. He came back a moment later with the towel, which had been soaked in water and twisted. This would give it weight, so it would hurt more—but wouldn't leave welts. They didn't want Sabra looking shabby for the customers.

—Now strip, bitch. You heard me. Take 'em off!

Sabra, cowed by the black fury in Angelo's eyes, did as commanded.

Now Angelo watched and cheered while Ken went to town on Sabra with the wet towel. He beat her all over her naked body, over and over, until he was tired.

When he was done, Angelo lay down on the bed. He was already hard from watching Ken beat Sabra.

—Suck it, he demanded.

Ken had his turn second. Sabra's first and most enthusiastic clients were her pimps and her jailors, and they never paid.

—You're working for us now, said Angelo, and you're going to work until you pay your airfare, food, rent and the clothes you just bought.

So it went. Sabra had no money and nowhere to go. Angelo let her know in no uncertain terms that if she tried to get away, she was a "dead pussy".

He had contacts in The Family. They would hunt her down, dismember her with chainsaws and bury her out in the desert. Nobody would hear her scream, nobody would ever know.

Chapter 13

The set up could not have been more convenient. Sabra's clients were sourced from Angelo's business customers. After slipping some extra cash, they were simply led from the garage to the spare bedroom inside the house.

Word got around, and soon Sabra was servicing guys from neighboring businesses on Colorado Street. Ken and Angelo divided the takings between them, passing nothing onto Sabra, who was now for all intents and purposes a sex slave.

If all this wasn't bad enough, Sabra had to service Ken and Angelo regularly for free as well.

At first, Sabra thought Angelo was the worst of the two. But soon, she wasn't so sure. At least with Angelo, you knew where you stood. He was the same all the time. He was always an asshole. Ken, on the other hand, would beat you and rape you and then say he was sorry, and buy you an ice cream.

Angelo's penchant for sodomy was renowned, but this was one thing Sabra resisted. She pointed out that she was too small. Angelo agreed, and threw a dildo at her.

—Get to work, he said, and loosen that thing up so I can use it.

* * *

One day the cousins had a novel idea to spin some real money. They would host a gangbang with Sabra and maybe one or two other girls. Angelo had contacts in a paper company out in Cudahy, a barren industrial district in Southeast Los Angeles. They would offer space at their box factory and supply customers from their employee pool.

One of Angelo's most devoted companions was Antoinette Lombardo, whose parents owned a Glendale hardware store. Antoinette was sixteen, young enough to get around on a bicycle, which she would ride over to Angelo's whenever she got the chance.

Angelo was her first love, and the man who took her virginity. Antoinette already knew she wanted to marry Angelo, even though she had never been with anyone else. By 1977 their liaison had already resulted in an abortion and a miscarriage. Angelo was tiring of Antoinette and her persistent talk of weddings, babies and other distasteful symbols of lifelong commitment.

—Listen darlin', Angelo said one day as they lay on his waterbed and he stroked her hair. How can I marry you if I don't know you would be faithful? And how do I know you can be faithful if you've never even been with another guy?

—That's crazy talk Angelo. I only want you.

Antoinette, at her tender age, didn't have a hope of catching his drift.

—But you might get to thinking you're missing out on something. And then you could run out on me. Honey, marriage is a real big deal.

If anyone would know it was Angelo; he'd already done it numerous times.

Angelo decided to offer Antoinette a deal. She should fuck someone else, and if she didn't like it, Angelo would marry her.

As it happened, Antoinette would have to have sex with more than one other man to prove her loyalty to Angelo. He decided she would pair with Sabra for the orgy at the box factory.

On the scheduled day, seven customers were waiting in line for the fun to begin. Amongst them were a number of high-ranking Los Angeles public officials, including the City Councilor of Bell and Police Chief of Huntington Park. Warren Schmucki, a chief aide to a member of the Los Angeles County Board of Supervisors, was also present.

The cousins raked in so much cash that day, they generously decided to give Sabra a small cut. Antoinette wasn't paid; fair punishment since she had, according to Angelo, apparently enjoyed herself. She was obviously a whore and would never make a fit wife, so into the bargain, he now had the perfect excuse not to tie the knot.

After the event, a resounding success for all concerned except Sabra and Antoinette, Ken and Angelo stood around in the parking lot with some of the town bigwigs to make small talk. Good cheer and backslapping abounded as the sun slipped down towards the skyline, enveloping them in all in the warm glow of a fine Los Angeles evening.

Ken noticed a decal with a Los Angeles county seal in the window of a vehicle in the parking lot. He learned the car belonged to Schmucki.

—Hey Mr. Schmucki, he said, deferential as ever. I've always been a real admirer of police and the work they do. What would a regular Joe like me have to do to get one of those decals?

Schmucki was on board. One slap on the back deserves another. He promised he'd arrange for Ken to get one of those decals, with the implicit proviso that Ken and Angelo keep the good times rolling.

* * *

Their wallets growing fatter by the day, Ken and Angelo decided it was time to add additional girls to their stable.

Angelo told Sabra that if she recruited another girl, they would let her go free. Sabra didn't know anyone in LA; all her friends were back in Phoenix. But she had an idea. There was going to be a Led Zeppelin concert in her hometown soon, and she was dying to go along with her friends. If they let her go, she would come back with another girl.

The trip back to Phoenix might have been the perfect opportunity for Sabra to escape. But she was deathly afraid of Angelo. When he told her his mob connections extended all over the country, and that she would be watched in Phoenix, she believed him. Sadly, she also believed him when he said that they would release her in exchange for another recruit. Sabra didn't want to be responsible for inflicting the life she'd been living on anyone else, let alone a friend, but she was so desperate she leapt on Angelo's offer.

Rebekah "Becky" Spears was to be the new girl on Ken and Angelo's books. Built like a glass of water, with long mousy blonde hair and a face whose intrinsic glumness told of an already less than pleasant existence, she had none of Sabra's bombshell appeal.

But to Angelo's delight, she proved more timid and compliant than her friend. Becky came from rough trade. The daughter of a biker, her expectations in life were already set low. She was hoping to leave her hard knock life in Phoenix behind. She was about to learn that moving to Los Angeles was a matter of taking three steps back.

Ken and Angelo knew that Sabra would be bitter when she realized that Angelo had tricked her about being freed, so they decided to offer a sweetener. They promised she would get a regular cut of the customer's fee from now on. They were going to go "professional". To this end, Angelo enlisted the cooperation of an associate, J.J. Fenway, who operated an outcall service called Foxy Ladies. The takings would be split between Fenway, Ken and Angelo, and the girl, whether Becky or Sabra. The bulk of the money of course went to Fenway, Ken and Angelo—Becky and Sabra received a pittance compared to the men. Meanwhile, they continued to service clients sourced through the trim shop for free.

There is nothing novel or unusual about Becky and Sabra's story. They, like thousands of other teenage runaways in Los Angeles, had been tricked and enslaved into prostitution by men operating under false pretenses. So common is this practice that these days billboards and digital displays warning kids about the dangers are dotted around bus stops, train stations, airports and other locations where pimps troll for runaways. Sadly, no such public awareness campaigns existed in the late seventies.

Life at Colorado Street was an unremitting nightmare for the girls. In between clients, Ken and Angelo made use of them whenever it took their fancy. Beatings and threats of grievous bodily harm and death were sufficient to ensure Becky and Sabra did their bidding and didn't try to escape.

Even so, Angelo had never succeeded in breaking Sabra into sodomy. Becky, on the other hand, acquiesced without argument. Angelo exploited this submissiveness so viciously and so often that he tore the muscles of her rectum, and she resorted to wearing a tampon in her anus to avoid soiling herself.

The horror seemed endless, so there was no way for them to know that at least one of them was about to get a lucky break.

One night, Becky was sent out on a call for Foxy Ladies. On what appeared to be just another miserable evening, the car snaked through dim streets and began to wind upwards. Looking out the window, Becky saw they were surrounded by the gated mansions of an opulent hillside suburb. Becky's client was David Wood, a wealthy Bel Air attorney.

All erotic thoughts disappeared from Wood's mind when he opened his door to find a thin and terrified teenager waiting outside. Becky looked so miserable and pathetic that Wood forsook the planned activities and sat with her talking, trying to comfort her.

Becky was so relieved that someone—anyone—was being nice to her that she let the cat out of the bag, and told Wood she and Sabra were being held hostage by two men down in Glendale. She thought they were cousins and their names were Ken and Angelo. Angelo, the older one, ran a car upholstery business from the rear of his house. She understood they were mixed up with the mob somehow. Becky said she and Sabra were in fear for their lives. They were being pimped out and raped and beaten and she was in no doubt that they would be killed if they tried to get away—or even if they didn't.

Wood wisely figured that these men were dangerous and violent criminals, and if he sent Becky back to them, particularly after she had just ratted them out, there was a good chance she would end up dead. He took Becky to the airport and put her on a flight back to Phoenix with nothing but the clothes on her back and a roll of bills.

When Becky never returned, Angelo called Foxy Ladies and had their driver take he and Ken to Wood's home in Bel Air. Finding nobody there, Angelo next called Wood's office and, when he got him on the phone, demanded he return Becky immediately or there would be hell to pay. Wood slammed down the receiver and went about his day. But he had a feeling that wouldn't be the last he heard from Buono, and he was right.

Ken and Angelo were fuming. Their girls were their property and their livelihood. More than that, their pride was injured. Becky had no business leaving them. They had been outsmarted by a lowly whore; such humiliation would not stand.

Angelo couldn't get to Becky so he made it his mission to take down David Wood, embarking on a campaign of intimidation and harassment.

Angelo always carried out his crusades with a creative touch. He threatened Wood with charges on underage sex and, when that failed to elicit a response, had flowers sent to all his staff with a note saying they had been terminated.

As an attorney, Wood had his own contacts in the criminal world. He got in touch with one of his clients, a part-time club bouncer built like a brick outhouse, and given the ironic nickname of Tiny.

A downside of Angelo's status as a businessman residing at the very base of his operations was that he was so easy to track down. One day, Angelo was working in his garage when five strange men appeared at his shop. Tiny had brought along some equally gargantuan associates for backup. Angelo, on sighting the men, gave no sign of distress and simply continued working as if they weren't even there.

Tiny didn't like this. Wood had already given him the rundown on Angelo and Ken and what they had been up to. These guys were scum, the lowest of bottomfeeders, and in Los Angeles that got pretty low.

Angelo's smug dismissiveness rubbed him the wrong way. Tiny walked over, stuck his meaty forearm through the window of the car and started pulling Angelo out through the window by his shirt collar.

Now Angelo was listening. Tiny picked him up by his arms and shook him round like a cocktail while he delivered his message. David Wood was his friend, and if Angelo ever messed with Wood again, he'd have Tiny to deal with.

Wood never heard from Buono again. Regardless, the cousins did not take these setbacks with good grace. With Becky gone, they worried that Sabra would get it in her head to take off next. They could have mutiny on their hands.

Fear was always the best weapon in their arsenal, so they went out and killed a cat, tossed its body into a cardboard box with some of Becky's clothes, presented it to Sabra, and hoped she'd get the hint. She'd be a dead pussy too if she tried any smart moves.

The warning didn't work. One day in September, Sabra vanished, never to return. She was so scared of Ken and Angelo that she immediately left California, and would not return until summoned there by the Los Angeles police in 1979.

The loss of Sabra had landed the death blow to Ken and Angelo's business. There was nothing coming in at all, and they were fending off irritable clients with lame excuses. Now the cousins were really dirty. Without money coming in from the girls Ken fell behind in his Cadillac repayments. They had to start from scratch, but they were eager to restart operations. They found a new girl to work for them, Jennifer Snyder, and set her up in the spare room in Angelo's house.

To expand their client base, they purchased a trick list from one Deborah Noble, a seasoned Hollywood prostitute Angelo met through his street connections. The list, containing the names and numbers of "verified" customers, cost Angelo $175. Angelo stressed to Deborah that he was only interested in men who wanted outcalls. Having guys see Jennifer in the house was one thing if they were Angelo's customers from the shop, but strangers was another story. He didn't want weirdos knocking on the door at Colorado Street at all hours.

Noble arrived at Angelo's garage to exchange the list for her payment accompanied by a tall, leggy black woman with an afro, decked out in clothing and jewelry that suggested she was making good money from her trade. Angelo made casual conversation with her for a while. The woman mentioned that her regular beat was around Sunset and Highland.

Angelo gave Jennifer the list and told her to get on the phone and start setting up appointments. She was not far into the task when she realized something wasn't right. All the men she spoke to expected to visit Jennifer at her place of work, not have her come to them. Deborah had knowingly taken money off Angelo for an in-call list, the very opposite of what he had asked for.

When Ken and Angelo realized that Noble had fucked them over, it was the final straw. They had hit their limit. Becky, Sabra, and now Deborah was making them a laughing stock. It was payback time. Someone had to set these smartass whores straight.

Ken's first instinct was to shoot the messenger. He immediately went into the spare bedroom and started tearing Jennifer's clothes off. But Jennifer fought back, digging her nails into him. Ken retreated back to the living room and ratted Jennifer out to Angelo for her disobedience.

Fuck Jennifer, said Angelo. His fury was focused on Deborah Noble. She had willfully screwed him in a business deal and he didn't like it one bit. Angelo wanted to go out and find Deborah and make an example of her, send a message loud and clear to all the cunts that Angelo was not to be messed with.

In the spare room, Jennifer hid away, scared of what might happen next. She heard Ken and Angelo talking loudly in the next room. She had never seen them so angry and was expecting a beating or worse.

Instead, suddenly there was silence. Ken and Angelo were gone. They were in Angelo's car driving out to Hollywood to look for Deborah, taking with them their fake badges and handcuffs with the intention of staging a false arrest.

Ken and Angelo cruised all the popular soliciting beats, but Deborah was nowhere to be found. But somewhere along the way, Angelo got the idea that they could send Deborah a message by getting to her friend. They turned and headed towards Sunset and Highland.

There, on the corner, just where she said she would be, was the tall black woman: Yolanda Washington.

PART THREE:
THE HOUSE OF MIRRORS

Chapter 14

On 28 March 1979, a little over a year after that night he and Angelo picked up and killed Yolanda Washington, Ken waited at the Whatcom county jail for his interview with Dr. Ronald Markman from the Los Angeles public defender's office, dwelling on the complexities of his situation.

His fortunes represented a rather mixed picture: certainly challenging, but not without room for optimism.

He was charged with murder, the highest penalty for which was death. Kelli continued to support him, but she couldn't deny the bare facts of the case set out before them, and neither could he. Meanwhile, his attorney and that kooky shrink John Watkins were telling him he might be crazy, a suggestion which, should it be proved true, could help him escape the worst punishment.

Nutty criminals were Markman's specialty. A qualified shrink plus a lawyer-in-training, he was destined to become America's most famous courtroom psychiatrist, and Charles Manson and the Symbionese Liberation Army were already entries on his CV. He would be helping the LA Public Defender with Ken's defense on the Los Angeles charges. He wasn't closed to the possibility of an MPD diagnosis but already had reservations, having seen many criminals attempt to evade justice on specious grounds of psychiatric illness. He would not use any hypnosis or regression techniques in his interview, and he was open to exploring other angles that might support Ken's innocence in the Los Angeles murders.

After Steve had first emerged under hypnosis shortly after Ken's arrest in January 1979, John Watkins suggested to Ken that "in time he would get to know the other 'part' of himself". In a therapeutic sense this instruction was meant to help Ken with the shock and trauma that would ensue when his conscious and moral self became aware of "Steve" and his criminal activities. Watkins had felt obliged to make it as a matter of professional duty of care. In a legal sense, however, the suggestion could give rise to new complications in the defense strategy.

Firstly, any later psychiatrist making a diagnosis would now reach a different conclusion, since Ken's "personalities" were becoming mutually aware, the barrier between them coming down. The MPD diagnosis safely referred to state of mind at the time of the crime, but it would only have Watkin's "say so", and was one shrink's say so enough? Second, if "Ken" became aware of "Steve" and his activities, this would impact the issue of Ken's competency to stand trial.

Dr. Markman's interview with Bianchi would indicate that these concerns were becoming a reality. An already vexing case was about to become a lot more complicated.

—Ken, Dr. Markman said, how do you feel about the possibility that you are guilty of killing those girls, Karen and Diane?

—Shock. Just … total shock.

—So you don't believe you did it?

—Well, if I were to learn a couple weeks back that I was responsible for those killings, I would probably go to pieces. Now I think I'm stronger. Now I would probably hold up better.

Ken explained that while before the knowledge that he had done something like that would have shattered him, he was now looking at it "as a real possibility" because of the facts and evidence in the case.

— I've been talking to Dean, and he said I might be sick. There might be something really wrong with me, mentally, you know?

Markman nodded, gesturing Ken to go on.

—And I said, no way. Not me. But then … lately I've been recalling some things from my past, times when I've had blank spots. Times where there is just a gaping hole in my memory and I should know what's gone on but I can't remember. I just feel there has been more to my life than I'm aware of ….

As Ken talked on and on about amnesia and his feeling that he was missing time, missing parts of himself, Markman was quietly mulling over the question that lay at the crux of the whole case. Was this guy the real deal, or was he just a sociopath committing a daring hoax?

While Bianchi opened up considerably about his childhood, reiterating the memories of abuse at the hands of his mother, Markman saw an opportunity.

He was scanning Ken's history for the routine clues of sociopathy, then thought to be bedwetting, arson and cruelty to animals. There was no record of Ken setting fire to property, and the bedwetting issue was obviously complicated. But a trait often found in sociopaths is the propensity to hurt or torture animals. Had he ever hurt animals on purpose?

No way! Ken was outraged at the suggestion that he would ever hurt an animal. He was very fond of pets, including his mother's cats when he was growing up.

—I remember this one time, I was driving … I ran over a cat. I went to see if it could be saved, it was gone, like … smoosh. Man, that bothered me for days.

Markman nodded sagely, but privately he was thinking about a record in Ken's file from Rochester that mentioned that as a teenager, Ken had once killed a cat and left it on a neighbor's porch as a Halloween prank.

This led to the next problem: Ken readily admitted to Markman that he was a chronic liar. It seemed that Ken had long learned the habit of deceit, of hiding himself, in order to get by; first with Frances, and then with anybody else who got close to him.

Kelli, Ken said, had often bore the brunt of his lies, but he himself was mystified by his senseless mendacity.

—It was as if I would open my mouth to say something, and something else altogether would fall out! I don't know why.

When Markman confronted Ken about the stolen goods found at the house in Bellingham, Ken openly admitted to taking them. He had considered at length the irony of a security guard moonlighting as a thief.

—It's weird, I know to sit here and talk to you now, that stealing is wrong. I preached not to steal. I mean that was my line of work, to pick up shoplifters!

Ken laughed, apparently amused by his own absurdity. He was flummoxed as to why he would steal four telephones, and admitted he had no use for them.

Bianchi continually referred to his criminal self as if it were a mysterious force he had no knowledge or control over.

—Why do I steal? Why do I lie? Beats the crackers out of me. I'm not normal. I'm not a normal person. For some reason there's … there's gotta be a reason why I lie, there's gotta be a reason why I steal. There's gotta be a reason for some of the things I've done…

Markman was perplexed. The man admitted to being a liar but he wanted everyone to believe the MPD was real. And really, it was a good argument: the lying was part of the same complex that had caused the MPD in the first place. The denial, the repression, the refusal to deal with reality, all springing from the history of abuse.

And, again, Ken had learned well throughout his life to please authority figures, to do and say what was expected of him. To what extent was whatever was happening in this semi-therapeutic exercise a product of that dynamic? Either way, the MPD angle of the case would likely not sustain if it was all a performance. The truth would come out.

And yet here he was, the dutiful patient, pledging he would do everything in his power to "get better". Ken insisted, despite his history of lying, that he was now trying so hard to leave all the lies behind. In order to heal, become a whole person, he knew he had to make a sincere effort to be completely open and honest and just put everything on the table.

—I'm working ... really working solidly on this one thing, to tell the truth no matter how much it hurts. No matter how it feels. Just be completely honest and open and truthful and I've never been that way.

—How do I know that's not a lie? asked Dr. Markman.

—Well, you don't. You're just gonna have to take my word for it.

* * *

At Watkin's suggestion, Ken had been keeping a diary and noting his dreams, thoughts and impressions. This was supposed to support him as he learned more about the hidden parts of himself. Whatever the therapeutic benefit of this exercise, it would not have been lost on Ken that Watkins, Brett and probably Judge Kurtz would be reading his notes.

On 30 March, two days after his interview with Markman, Ken recorded in his journal a memory of what appeared to be a dissociative episode. He was visiting the house of a childhood friend, when suddenly he found himself sitting on the front steps of the house, with no idea how he got there. His friend and the family were gone, and he didn't know where they went or how long it had been since they left. Bianchi also wrote that, this same night, after going to sleep at the normal time he had awoken in the night lying on the floor of his cell next to the toilet.

Watkins and Dean Brett perused these entries and saw further evidence that Ken suffered MPD. Taken together with the evidence gathered from the hypnotic session with Watkins, their confidence was growing that they had a new angle on their case.

Now, following his confession to Dr. Markman that he was beginning to accept the possibility that he—as "Steve"—had murdered the girls in Washington, and further discussing his situation with Dean Brett, Bianchi was suddenly willing to reconsider the matter of his plea. On 30 March, Dean Brett made it known to the court that the defense would be lodging a plea of not guilty by reason of insanity.

Judge Kurtz of course saw that whether or not Kenneth Bianchi actually suffered Multiple Personality Disorder was a crucial matter in determining whether he was fit to stand trial, and he was not satisfied on the basis of Watkins' report alone. He decided it was necessary to bring in additional experts to evaluate Bianchi. In the end, a total of six psychiatrists would assess Ken. Two, including Watkins, were paid by the defense, two were appointed as impartial advisers to Judge Kurtz, and two worked for the prosecution.

* * *

When the Los Angeles investigators learned of the developments in Bellingham they were horrified, but not surprised. They knew when they saw Ken's performance for Watkins during the hypnosis session that he had begun working the angle of an insanity plea, and now it was clear that his defense team had fallen for it; either that or they were happy to run with it either way.

Despite their disappointment at this turn of events they were following the developments with great interest. Bianchi, as "Steve", had divulged concrete details about Angelo Buono that tied him to the Los Angeles murders. He had described the Colorado Street residence and business, the Yolanda Washington murder, and had mentioned locations near freeways where bodies had been found. The detectives were sure that Ken was faking MPD, but they also held a strong suspicion that his testimony regarding Buono was entirely accurate.

Even so, it was in no way sufficient to justify an arrest. All the officers could do for now was maintain their surveillance of Buono until hard evidence that lined up with Bianchi's confession was uncovered. The cops were nervous, because if Buono was indeed the other Hillside Strangler, and he was free, there was a chance he could kill again. They couldn't arrest Buono yet, but they contemplated the possibility of leaking to the media Buono's status as a suspect. At least this way the public would know to be wary of him. On the other hand, what if it turned out Angelo wasn't involved in the Hillside murders? Many innocent people had already suffered as a result of the investigation, and they didn't want to make any more mistakes. They hesitated over their next move.

In the meantime, Salerno—now armed with photographs of the two suspects—once again sought out Markust Camden. He tracked him down to Indiana, where he learned Camden had been staying at Richmond State Hospital, a mental health facility. It turned out Camden had checked himself in voluntarily after problems with his latest partner caused some kind of breakdown. Over the phone, Salerno found Camden lucid and cooperative, and he was able to convince him to take a flight out to California for another interview.

The two met at the Gala Inn in downtown Los Angeles in early April 1979, where Salerno showed Camden two spreads of mug shots, one including a photo of Bianchi, the other a shot of Buono. Camden didn't react when shown the picture of Bianchi, but immediately picked Buono from the second spread of shots.

—That's the guy, he said. That's the guy I seen leave with Judy at the railroad diner.

—Would you be willing to repeat that under oath?

—I most certainly would.

There was a problem though. Camden's recent stay in a mental institution would likely tarnish his credibility as a witness. Salerno was convinced that Camden's memory and cognitive capacities were fine as far as identifying Buono, but a jury couldn't know that.

Beulah Stofer was also a problematic witness due to her eyesight problems. But now Detective Grogan visited her once again to see if she could pick Buono or Bianchi out of a spread of mug shots. She seemed as poorly as ever, and began wheezing immediately when Grogan produced the photographs. Nonetheless she picked both Bianchi and Buono out of the mug runs as the men she had seen abducting Lauren Wagner.

Beulah, however, still would not admit that she had gone outside her house to take a look, and a jury would never believe that she had seen the men well enough to identify them from inside her house, with her failing vision and in a dark environment. Grogan also doubted that she was actually physically well enough to take the stand.

Despite these concerns, there was mounting excitement in Los Angeles. The investigative team now had two independent witnesses who had seen Buono, Bianchi or both in the company of Hillside victims in the period immediately before their disappearance and death. They were now certain they had their men, and the legal proof was not far behind.

Chapter 15

In Washington, once Judge Kurtz received the defense's plea of not guilty by reason of insanity, he appointed Ralph Allison, an expert in Multiple Personality Disorder from Davis, California, to assess Ken and act as an independent adviser.

At the time of his first meeting with Bianchi, Allison was writing what would become an authoritative text on MPD, *Minds in Many Pieces*. He had moderated programs at the American Psychiatric Association on multiples, and was a foremost expert in his field, having developed techniques for diagnosing MPD based on an apparently sound empirical system drawing on years of painstaking research. The only real problem was that the patients Allison had studied were not, generally speaking, criminals facing the death penalty. His diagnostic techniques did not prepare him for the complex forensic situation that lay ahead.

Allison would assess Bianchi twice, first in April 1979, and then again in June. He decided the only way he could make a diagnosis was to compare Bianchi to other cases he had known, which to his mind meant asking him to act like a patient. He would later declare that he was aware of the risks of treating Ken as a patient in the forensic setting when he was "not under contract to be his therapist", but he saw no other way to achieve his task.

Allison interviewed Ken on 18 April. Prior to this, he had the opportunity to review the transcripts of the sessions with Watkins, Ken's various medical reports including that from the DePaul psychiatric clinic, and Ken's prison journal. A number of entries in the journal, in particular, were of great interest to Allison.

During the first half of April, after his interview with Dr. Markman, Ken reported in his diary that at times he would arrive at Angelo's house and Angelo would speak to him or give him a look as if they had shared something he didn't remember. On 1 April he dreamed that he was at Angelo's house surrounded by naked girls who "who didn't appear to move". He felt a nudge and looked down and found himself sitting on a girl. He heard cries from the spare bedroom and then he woke up.

During this same week, Ken noted in his diary that the name "Steve" had popped up several times in his mind, but he didn't link the name to any individual in particular, and on 15 April, he described a dream in which he struggled with a hostile entity that "looks like me but is not me."

Allison wrote in his notes that this dream had taken place before his first session with Ken, but after Watkins' visit, and appeared to be following Watkins' post-hypnotic suggestion that he become aware of Steve in a safe fashion and in his own time. Allison observed that it had taken about three weeks for him to have this awareness following the visit by Dr. Watkins, implying he thought the delayed emergence of Ken's awareness of Steve meant that it was unlikely he was malingering.

On 17 April, Ken wrote the following poem:

I'm scared
My stomach hurts
There's no place to run now,
It was so easy to run away before.
I feel strong, in control but still unsure
of someone I have come to know,
someone I don't understand as well as I know myself
... now.
If only I could understand what brought us together.
I am so alone now, somewhat I feel naked.
I'm knowing me.
I wish I were free of him. I want help,
I don't care for him
And he doesn't like me. I feared confinement but
I am thankful for it now.

Allison was amazed by what he was reading. Following the work that Watkins had done with him already, Ken Bianchi was clearly undergoing the typical early stages of the transformation of consciousness that occurs when an individual becomes aware of his alter or alter personalities. He had seen these kinds of signs and signals over and over again in his observations of previous patients. Typically they would be subtle at first, because the process of recognizing one's alters could pose a tremendous challenge to the personality. Dreams about the alter, or about experiences undergone while in the alter personality state, would be very common during this transformation process, since dreams were a gentle way for the subconscious to nudge the conscious mind towards accepting the existence of the "others". Such dreams typically signaled that the beginning of the transformation process was underway.

There was something else too: something that Allison regarded as even more significant.

In this same batch of journal entries, dated 17 April, Ken recorded a dream of playing with his imaginary friend Sticks, whom Ken described as a twin brother.

I was playing with my twin Sticks ... on either Ravine or Villa Street. We were running down the street, playing games, laughing; we shared a lot ... mother came to the front door of our house and called me to come into the house, but she didn't call my brother. I went in and tried to explain that he was still outside, she wouldn't let me finish what I was saying; she slapped me and sent me to my room ...

Ken had lived at Villa Street when he was around eight years old. Allison opined that Sticks started out as Ken's supporter. He was a healthy part of Ken's mind, projected as an imaginary friend, which rejected Mrs. Bianchi's efforts to control and abuse Ken. But Ken, in his efforts to satisfy his mother, had rejected Sticks, who then "split off" and gradually turned into the hostile entity "Steve".

Allison was excited by his discovery, but—in his mind at least—it wasn't as if he had simply been carried away, and ignored the possibility that Ken was manufacturing his MPD symptoms via his prison journal. The reason? Kenneth Bianchi had undergone IQ testing and only managed a score of 116. This was only on the slightly bright end of average; certainly not clever enough to have, of his own initiative, located, read and understood the kind of research materials he would have had to access to know exactly what signs and symptoms to mimic to make these venerable experts of their field think he had MPD.

As for the imaginary playmate—that wasn't well documented in commonly available literature at all. How could Ken have known that most children who will grow to suffer the syndrome have them?

Allison therefore assumed that the only starting point Ken would have had for any "performance" was the post-hypnotic suggestion made by Watkins. And that alone wasn't enough to justify the very specific signs that Ken was showing, signs that Allison had seen many times in his patients.

* * *

Allison came to the session on 18 April with many questions, but uppermost in his mind was the matter of what had been happening when Ken was around eight or nine, living at Villa Street. Whatever that was, Allison thought, probably underlay the psychic break that had created the second entity, Steve.

In order to learn more, Allison performed an age regression technique on Ken that involved putting him into a hypnotic state and then counting backwards to the age at which the causes of present difficulties occurred. The patient could then talk about whatever had happened at that age without interference or repression from the conscious mind.

The regression was performed in a guarded room with both Dean Brett and John Johnson present. Johnson recorded the session on a handheld camera, and the resulting tape was to become notorious in both the legal and mental health fields.

After placing Ken "under" with a guided relaxation technique, Allison counted from zero to 27, instructing Ken to "allow" his left index finger to rise off the desk whenever Allison mentioned an age at which important events related to the present situation occurred. Ken raised his left finger at ages nine and thirteen. Once Allison reached Ken's present age of 27 he counted back downwards.

—Ken, let yourself get younger as I count back down and to be that age ... you will be able to talk about whatever was going on for you at that time by reliving it, or seeing it, or any way that feels okay to you...

When Allison counted back down to nine, Ken started speaking. It wasn't Ken's normal speaking voice, but this was not "Steve" either. The voice was that of a child.

—Mom and Dad are fighting.

—Uh-huh, Allison said. What are they fighting about?

—Because mommy hits me.

—Hits you?

—I hate it. I don't want her to hit me. I just want to run away. I run outside or I go and hide. I want to get away. I try, I try so hard, to stay on her good side…

—And what do you have to do to stay on her good side?

—I always gotta do whatever Mommy says. But it's never enough. Whatever I do, she gets mad anyway. She's always picking on me. On Dad too. She's always yelling and screaming. She just can't talk like a normal person. She's gotta yell and scream all the time.

—How does that affect you, Ken? When Mommy yells at you and hits you?

—I want to die. I don't want her to be my Mommy anymore.

"Child" Ken whined slightly, as if holding back tears between words. To Allison's mind, the hurt and fear of child Ken, struggling to cope with this chaotic and abusive relationship with the mother, was almost palpable.

Allison knew Ken had just turned nine, so he asked Ken how he had spent his birthday.

—I wanted my friends to come over. I wanted to have a cake. But Mommy was mad at me, so I didn't have a birthday party.

Poor Ken, thought Allison. Such intense loneliness and isolation. Ken told him that most of the time the other kids didn't want to come near him because they were scared of Frances.

—She's only mad at me and Dad, but they don't understand. They're afraid of her. Mommy keeps everyone away from me.

Allison asked Ken how he was surviving, how he handled it when Frances yelled at him and hit him.

—I hide. I like hiding. It's easy to hide from everything. I hide under my bed, in my closet, behind the house. The bed is the best place.

* * *

Now Allison asked a most controversial question that had, by his own admission, a rather leading quality; but to his mind he needed to ask if it were to learn the origins of Steve.

—Did you ever hide inside your own head?

—Yeah. Sometimes. To get away.

—What happens in there?

—I talk to Steve.

—Who's Steve?

—He's my friend.

—Does he have a last name?

Bianchi hesitated, and Allison asked the question again. Ken then mumbled something barely intelligible. On subsequent replays of the recording, the name sounded like "Walker."

—Where'd he get that name? Who are Steve's parents?

—Steve didn't have a mom and dad. Stevie was alone.

—And how did you meet Steve?

—I ran away from Mommy, she was hitting me so hard. I ran and hid under the bed. I was crying in the dark. I closed my eyes and when I opened them suddenly Stevie was there. He said, "Hi. I'm your friend."

Ken was so happy to finally have a friend. He and Stevie played together, and they both liked to hide. But Stevie hated Frances. He told Ken to hit her back, or run away from home, but Ken was too afraid.

—I couldn't hit her. I couldn't run away. She loves me. I love her.

—But Stevie doesn't love her.

—No. He doesn't want anything to do with her.

Steve lived with Ken, slept in Ken's bed, and they wore the same clothes, except Stevie wore his shirt un-tucked, where Ken wore his shirt inside his pants, like his mother wanted. Stevie didn't like school, but he was smarter than Ken. He loved to play practical jokes on people, like jumping out from behind a tree to scare them. Ken didn't do things like that; he thought it was a little cruel.

Steve's personal characteristics, his rebellious nature, all made perfect sense to Dr. Allison based on what he had seen in other patients. Clearly Ken had created Steve to protect him from Frances. Alters emerge to help an individual cope with conditions of extreme trauma. In Ken's case the aggressive part of himself that defended his ego had split away, since taking ownership of those aggressive impulses exposed Ken to danger from his mother.

But all this came at a price; Ken could be blamed for Steve's transgressions. After all, it would be Ken that got punished if Steve wore his shirt on the outside. And it would be Ken that got the gas chamber if Steve killed somebody.

Resuming the regression technique, now Allison counted up to age thirteen. Ken said his parents were still fighting constantly, and now the neighbors were at it too. Ken hated all the yelling and wanted to run away.

—Where is Steve now?

—I don't see much of Stevie. Steve and I aren't really friends anymore.

—Why?

—Stevie's angry with me. He doesn't understand why I put up with it all.

—Well, where is Stevie now?

—I don't know. He just went away. Once in a while he comes back. But it isn't the same anymore. We used to be such good friends.

—How come you aren't friends anymore?

—Stevie isn't funny anymore. He's mean.

Ken said that he was starting to like girls and that Steve liked girls too, but only in a certain way. Steve liked to hurt girls, and Ken didn't understand that at all.

—How does he hurt the girls?

—Punches 'em. He told me he knocked one girl down on the sidewalk. Stevie gets his kicks hurting girls. He thinks it's really great.

—Well if he's mean, maybe it's better he's gone away.

—Maybe. But now I'm all alone with Mom. Now that Daddy's gone...

Allison knew that Ken's father passed recently. With Nicholas gone, Frances' emotional dependence on Ken would have increased, no doubt an additional stress on the personality that was, in Allison's opinion, likely very significant.

—He just went to work one day, said Ken, and he was dead. Why did he leave me?

—What do you think made your father go away?

—God wanted him more than we did. But I really needed him. Now I'm alone with Mommy.

—How does that feel?

—She always wants me home. I can't be Dad. I keep telling her I can't be Dad. I'm just a kid...

Chapter 16

Allison was satisfied, based on what he had just seen, that his hypothesis about the origins of Ken's problems was correct. Childhood abuse, compounded by the death of Ken's father, were the crucial events underlying the present crisis. The existence of a dissociative syndrome was clearly suggested by the history of an imaginary playmate that had started as Ken's helper but later turned into a powerful, hostile entity that eventually posed a threat to the core personality itself.

And there was something else: while Ken was under, Allison had seen him shaking his head from side to side, a recurrence of the "purposeless movements" seen by doctors in Ken's childhood. Allison knew these as "psychological automatisms". He would point out in his report to the court that they had been observed and studied extensively in cases of MPD. The movements, he explained, appear "purposeless" but are in fact "highly symbolic and meaningful from the unconscious psychological standpoint of the patient".

Next Allison wanted to try to speak to Steve directly, to establish Steve's existence at the later time relevant to Bianchi's legal difficulties and what role, if any, he had played in the murder of the young women in Washington.

This would be Allison's first encounter with the infamous alter. Steve's reputation for lashing out preceded him, so Allison was on guard. He didn't know quite what to expect, or even if he could get Steve to appear. He counted forward in time, to Ken's present age of 27, and asked for Steve to "come out" and talk.

All went smoothly; certainly, in the opinion of the Los Angeles investigators who later watched the tape, rather too smoothly.

At Allison's instruction, Bianchi's head immediately jerked and his eyes opened.

—What?

—Hello? Who's that?

—Steve.

—What's your last name?

Steve didn't answer. He lunged out of his chair towards Johnson, operating the camera.

—You! You're the motherfucker that's been trying to get me to leave him!

Allison was unsettled, but gave no outward sign of alarm. He was guiding the session, and it was his job to keep things under control.

—You can't do that, he said evenly.

He motioned Steve back to his chair with his finger.

—Fuck! Fucker...

The volley of expletives continued as Steve flailed about the room, eventually landing back in his chair.

—What's your last name? Allison repeated.

—The fuck business is it of yours!?

Steve, or Ken, apparently didn't like this question.

—I'm just trying to find out who I'm talking to. How old are you Steve?

—Why? What are you, writing a fuckin' book or something?

—No, I'm writing a report for the judge, Allison said drily.

—Well fuckin' ask him then!

Steve seemed unaware of the gravity of his—or Ken's—situation. This might or might not have been significant in terms of the question of state of mind at the time of the crime. Allison wanted to explore this further.

—You do realize, don't you, that you are charged with two counts of murder in the state of Washington? That you are to appear before the judge?

—Fuck off.

—I know that Ken is 27 years old. Are you 27?

—That fuckin' asshole. Fuck him.

"Steve" pulled a packet of cigarettes out of his shirt front pocket and, with a slight sense of ceremony, took one from the packet and ripped the filter off.

—The ashtrays are on the chair over there ... Allison offered helpfully.

—I know where the fuckin' ashtrays are! You don't have to tell me!

Steve grabbed an ashtray, lit his cigarette and stalked back to his chair.

—You're all a bunch of fuckin' assholes, you know that?

—How so?

—Before, I could come out whenever I wanted. Now you gotta stick your fuckin' nose in this whole shittin' business! I was doin' fine ... now I can't even come out when I want to!

—Well, what's stopping you?

—That fuckin' asshole. Forget it ... just fuckin' forget it.

Allison took it that "that fuckin' asshole" referred to Ken, and that Ken—largely useless and powerless, according to Steve—was not completely useless, since he stood in the way of the gratification of Steve's murderous desires, by preventing Steve getting out and interacting with the world whenever he felt like it.

—You've been here a while now ... three months isn't it? Have you ever come out here, in prison?

The question of whether Steve had been able to "get out" since Ken was arrested was a good one, but it probably would have been better to ask the prison staff if they had noticed anything unusual about Ken's behavior, any dramatic changes. Unbeknownst to Allison, in the time Bianchi had been incarcerated, none of the guards or anyone else he had interacted with in prison had ever met "Steve".

—Yeah, I fuckin' used to! I did anything I fuckin' wanted. I want that fucker gone. He's been a hassle to me all my life.

—In what way?

—He's such a goody two-shoes. Once upon a time I actually used to like that asshole.

—You two used to be good friends.

—Yeah, used to be ... he just fuckin' won't listen! You know, there's a fuckin' right way to do things, and there's my way to do things, and my way's always been the right fuckin' way to do things! Fuck 'em. Nobody's worth shit out there. It's just a fucked-up world!

—Well, I'd have to agree with you there...

—Just, fuck him. And fuck his mother too.

Fuck his mother. Now Allison saw a helpful opening. He wanted to get Steve talking about Mrs. Bianchi; after all, it was looking to him that there was a clear relationship between Steve's hatred of Frances and his later desire to hurt and kill women.

—She was quite the bitch wasn't she? Allison goaded.

—She was a fuckin' cunt! He still puts up with her shit … fuck man, he has got to wise up, you know? He just … I want to get out, I want to stay out, and, fuck it, that's all there is to it. I'm just a better person than him.

—But … you have gotten yourself into kind of a jam, haven't you?

Steve seemed so thoroughly convinced he was smarter than Ken. And yet he didn't seem to grasp that what happened to Ken, would happen to him as well.

—Nah, he got himself into a jam. Yeah, I killed those broads, you know, to smarten him up. To show him I can't be messed with.

—Which broads?

—Those two fuckin' cunts. That blonde cunt and the brunette cunt!

—Why did you kill them?

—'Cos I hate fuckin' cunts!

Allison wanted to know why it had been Karen Mandic and Diane Wilder specifically.

—No real reason. All cunts are the same. He knew 'em, that's all.

—Oh? I thought Ken only knew Karen a little.

—He knew one of them. The other one came along for the ride. Cunts are so fuckin' stupid!

—Okay. How did you do it?

—I strangled 'em. I strangled 'em with a cord. Nuthin' to it…

—Did you bring the cord or was it there at the house?

—You bet, dope, brought it with me from my basement.

—And how did you get them to Dr. Catlow's?

—Hah. It was a fuckin' cinch, man. He's such a sap. He left, I came. I called Karen. I set it up so she could bring her girlfriend. I offered them a couple hundred.

—That's quite a lot of money.

—It's a sap deal, man! I never even had cash to pay them!

Steve laughed heartily, amused at how easily he had tricked the girls.

—Why did you kill the girls? Allison asked.

—Because I was trying so hard to get out, where I belong. I want to be out. I want him gone, out of the way. I belong out in the world where I can do whatever I fuckin' want to.

Steve apparently wanted to do away with Ken so as to be in sole possession of the body. This was something Allison had encountered before in cases of

MPD. Steve's reasoning seemed to be that Ken would get done for the crime, and somehow this would free Steve.

—And supposing you succeeded in 'getting him out of the way'... what do you think would happen to you?

Steve, seemingly blindsided, silently pondered the question a while.

—Nuthin' would happen to me.

—How did you expect him to disappear? By being executed?

Steve was again silent.

—Did it ever occur to you that that body there, Allison pointed at Steve, might be executed by the law for first-degree murder?

—So fuckin' what?

Steve still wasn't following.

—Well, that would sort of put an end to a lot of the, ah, activity, would it not?

—I guess, Steve conceded.

—Did you consider that before you killed those girls?

—Fuck, no!

Allison had seen with previous patients that alters often had an unrealistic understanding of the world. Because their purpose was to give expression to the cut off, repressed and impulsive parts of a person, and they lacked the organizational functions of the ego, they suffered from magical thinking, and didn't perceive cause and effect. So all of this was making perfect sense to him in terms of his understanding of the syndrome.

A more skeptical view might be that Steve's confusion illustrated that Bianchi had not prepared a comprehensive strategy for fooling the doctor—his story had some "holes" in it.

—Did you think about whether it was right or wrong to kill them?

—No way was it wrong! Why is it wrong to get rid of some fuckin' cunts?

—Why is it right?

—Because it makes the world a better place to live in!

Steve was finally on firmer ground.

—Did you know that there was a law against killing people, killing girls?

—Fuck laws. Laws are nuthin' but writing on paper!

—Did you realize there is a law, on paper, that says...

—Fuck, no!

—Did you know that Washington has a law that says you get executed if you happen to go around killing girls?

—That's bullshit!

—I'm afraid it isn't.

Steve's frustration was mounting. Arguing with reason was not for him.

—I don't know why I fuckin' talk to you, man. This asshole over here is trying to get rid of me, this one over there is trying to get rid of me … and you got all the questions!

—That's right, I'm just asking you some questions, that's my job. Nobody can get rid of you except Ken.

—Hey, let me clue you in, man. It's a fucked job you got.

—That's true…

—You really should get out and live a little.

—My wellbeing is not your concern, Steve.

—Yeah you're right, I forgot.

Allison wanted to steer Steve back to topic.

—So, down in Los Angeles, with Angelo? Is that your idea of living? Hmm?

—Oh yeah. He's my kinda person.

—Mm? What's so great about this Angelo?

—He just doesn't give a fuck. He really doesn't give two fucks about life, mine or yours. That's good. That's a good attitude to have.

—Uh-huh … has he killed anybody?

—Oh, yeah.

—How many?

—Five. He done five cunts down in LA.

—Did you see this? Did you watch?

—You bet I did! I wasn't going to miss that.

—You're sure he killed five girls?

—Positively … without a doubt.

—And what about you, did you kill any girls down in LA?

—Yep, I did. Four of 'em.

—Okay, that makes nine.

Allison knew the count of the Los Angeles victims. Steve's numbers weren't adding up.

Steve seemed much calmer now, as if soothed by distant and sweet memories.

—What a team we were…

—Sure sounds like it. You two were quite busy, weren't you? What time period was this happening over?

—It was a while back. Over a couple of years, maybe a year.

—When you were living with Angelo?

—No, it started after I moved out...

—Okay. And how did you kill them?

—Strangled 'em all. With cords. It's the best way to go. Nuthin' to it.

—Did you bring them with you?

—Bags ... you bet!

—What do you mean, "bags"?

—Cellophane bags. You twist 'em up real tight. Nuthin' fuckin' to it. Angelo had everything. He had all kinds of shit in his shop. Bags, cords...

This was the first Allison, or anyone, had heard about the use of plastic bags in the killings. Steve's rather visual description of "twisting them real tight" seemed to imply that they had been used as asphyxiation devices in conjunction with the ligatures. Allison felt sick as he pictured a deathtrap crafted from cellophane and cord tightening around a girl's neck. Bianchi and Buono had really applied themselves to their work. Those poor women never stood a chance.

Even so, this information, if it could be corroborated, would prove to be very useful to the detectives in California. Assuming Steve wasn't lying, he had just told them that they should be looking in Buono's shop for a match to any physical evidence lifted from the bodies. Of that there was a paucity; but there had been the piece of fluff lifted from Judy Miller's eyelid, and the traces of adhesive found on Lauren Wagner's wrists.

—Okay. So what about this Angelo? Why did he want to kill girls?

—I don't know man, he was just an easy guy to get with the program, you know? I gave him the idea, and he went with it all the way, you know, he's my kinda person! We should have more people like that in the world, then we'd have less problems...

—Well, how did you decide to kill girls in the first place?

—We were sitting around shootin' the shit one day, and I asked him, just out of nowhere, if he'd ever killed anybody. He thought he was talking to Ken, you see...

—Uh-huh...

—He thought nuthin' of it. He said, why do you want to know? I said, well what does it feel like? He said, I don't know. And I said, we should find out sometime. So we did!

Allison asked how long had it had been after this conversation that they had taken their first victim. Steve started talking about the Yolanda Washington murder, for which he took the credit.

—Some black broad. We picked her up downtown. She was by the side of the road. She was a hooker. Angelo got her in the car. We got on the freeway. I fucked her, and killed her. We dumped her body off. That was it. Nuthin' to it.

—You fucked her first?

—That's right.

—Did it feel good?

—You bet it did. We fucked 'em all first. That's all they're worth, man. That's all they're good for.

—Okay. Who killed the second one?

Allison referred to Judy Miller.

—Angelo. He did a real nice job of it too.

—Did he fuck her too?

—He sure the fuck did, and so did I.

—Okay. And where did you kill her?

—In Angelo's house. Actually, all the cunts died in Angelo's house. It's a great pad he's got there.

—Sounds like quite a place...

More useful information. Steve pointed to the house at Colorado Street as the scene of the crimes.

—So when the killing stopped, how did it stop?

—How the fuck do I know?

—Was it because Ken moved, up here?

—I wanted to kill more broads. But him, he's got ... you know, fuck him man, I don't want him to fight me...

—Is there anybody else in there who fights you, besides Ken?

Allison here tried to establish the existence of any other alters, apart from Steve.

—No, just him.

—And the girls you killed up here, did you fuck them too?

—Yep, fucked 'em both.

—They were found fully clothed, no? How did you do it?

Allison knew that the MO in the Washington murders was markedly different to the LA killings, in which all the victims were found naked. He was trying to learn more about this.

—Well, they didn't have their clothes on when I fucked 'em! How you gonna fuck a broad with her clothes on? Make some fuckin' sense, man. What are you, a kid? I fucked 'em, made 'em get dressed, then I killed 'em!

—Both of them at the same time?

Steve was losing patience with the doctor's questions. This learned man had no common sense at all.

—No! Separately! I tied 'em up … had 'em in separate places … killed one, killed the other. Understand?!

—Which room did you have the first one in?

—In the bathroom. That was Diane Wilder. The brunette. Flat-chested girl. Fucks really bad.

—And where was the other girl, Karen?

—In the downstairs bedroom … she was a nice cunt, that broad.

—You strangled them?

—Yep. I carried 'em out, put 'em in the car, drove the car to that cul-de-sac … nuthin' fuckin' to it.

—What street was the cul-de-sac on?

—How the fuck should I know? I just drove around 'til I found a fuckin' street…what am I supposed to do, stop and read fuckin' street signs? Will you make some sense now? You know, if you're gonna fuckin' talk to me, make some fuckin' sense!

Steve rose out of his chair and went for Johnson again.

—Turn that shit off! I want to be out! I want to be out!

This seemed like a good time to end the session.

—Okay, you can go back to where you came from…

—I don't want to…

—Ken's gonna have to come out…

—I want to stay now…

—Ken's gonna have to come out … come out Ken! Ken, come out! … Ken!

Allison raised his right hand and pushed it towards Steve's face. Steve slumped back into his chair, closed his eyes, and when he opened them, Ken was staring out.

He looked down at the cigarette in his hand, apparently bewildered.

—When did I take this out of my packet?

—You were in a trance, Allison said helpfully.

—I don't remember taking it out of my pack. Someone has broken the filter off!

Ken was lost in wonder.

—You don't break off the filter?

—Oh no. I can't smoke an unfiltered cigarette...

Chapter 17

The unfiltered Camel was just the cherry on the sundae. Ralph Allison had already made up his mind. He concluded Kenneth Bianchi was legally insane at the time of the Washington killings, and because of the amnesia for the time period of the offenses, was unable to stand trial. He completed his report to Judge Kurtz accordingly.

This was excellent news for Ken, and there was more to come. A series of inkblot tests ordered by Dr. Watkins had been sent away for expert analysis, and the results that came back also suggested that Ken suffered from Multiple Personality Disorder.

Dr. Watkins administered two tests on Bianchi, one on the conscious and self-aware "Ken", and one on the alter "Steve", while Ken was (apparently) under hypnosis.

Watkins sent the test results to Dr. Erika Fromm, a psychology professor from the University of Chicago. Fromm knew nothing about the Bianchi case or even that the inkblot tests were taken from the same individual; Dr. Watkins had labeled the tests simply as "Mr. K" and "Mr. S" as if they had indeed been administered on two different people—which in Watkins' view, they actually had.

The results were interesting, whether you thought Ken was a multiple or not. Mr. K described the following images in the inkblot series: people dancing at a disco; children playing on London Bridge; two men carrying a bucket; a butterfly; a snail; a moth; a steamboat on a river; two little Indians; a leopard; rocks beside a pond; the Asian continent; two dogs fighting over a bone; and an unborn fetus.

Dr. Fromm concluded from Mr. K's Rorschach test that the subject was "a near normal man" despite mild traits of neuroticism and introversion. She felt the test results indicated he was, however, prone to fantasy and daydreaming, perhaps possessing a degree of "repressed creative ability".

Mr. S, on the other hand, was beyond pathological. Dr. Fromm stated in her report that his was the sickest Rorschach she had seen in the four decades she had been interpreting the tests. He saw "two elephants fucking each other", "a big dick", "two broads getting it on" and "an abortion." The patient, wrote Dr. Fromm, was an individual in whose mind sexuality and violent aggression against women were intimately joined. He was likely a rapist and a killer, she cogently remarked, with an aside that society's needs would best be served by ensuring such a man was safely sequestered in a prison or state hospital.

Dr. Watkins seized on Fromm's comments as further proof that Bianchi was a multiple, not taking seriously the possibility that he had deliberately staged his responses on the test to produce the appearance of two drastically different personalities.

Dr. Watkins concurred with Allison that Bianchi was not clever enough to pull such a ruse. Sure, he had taken some primer courses in psychology in Rochester before he dropped out of college; and some psychology textbooks had been found in the house in Bellingham after Ken's arrest. It was Watkins' opinion that these were nothing more than relics of his student days. Supporting this interpretation were statements made by Kelli Boyd. She said that for the entire time she lived with Ken, he had rarely opened a book of any kind. To test this out, Watkins had even taken it upon himself to discuss with Ken a chapter he himself had written in one of the books that was found at the house. Watkins' had found that it was completely beyond Bianchi's comprehension.

Watkins was so confident in his diagnosis that he struck a deal with *Time* for an exclusive interview expounding on the MPD theory of the Hillside Strangler. The resulting article was published on 7 May 1979. In it, Watkins asserted that the normally sensitive and gentle Bianchi was inhabited by an "evil doppelganger", and that Ken had no memory of anything that happened to him, or anything he did, while under the influence of the sinister alter "Steve".

For Ken, an acquittal for the Washington murders on the basis of insanity was now looking like a good possibility. Two eminent psychiatrists were convinced that Ken was suffering from Multiple Personality Disorder. If they were so sure, who was he to argue?

Ken wrote letters to Kelli filling her in on all the good news. He promised her the whole terrible nightmare would soon be over, and they would be reunited, one happy little family, just like they had been before. Ken seemed particularly excited about the article in *Time*. Maybe there would be a book deal on the horizon? They could cash in and get famous.

Ken didn't want little Ryan forgetting his father, so he made cassettes of himself cooing baby talk, enclosing them with his letters.

The tapes, and Ken's letters, brought up painfully ambivalent feelings for Kelli. She knew how desperately sad Ken was, being separated from his son. He adored Ryan, there was no doubt about that. She still loved Ken, and whatever troubles they had had in the past, she didn't want him locked up in prison for the rest of his life. The multiple personality theory bothered her though. She was no psychiatrist, but she wasn't aware of the amnesic lapses that Ken claimed to have suffered from for as long as he could remember. Certainly though, she herself had sometimes felt that Ken was almost two different people; one, loving and kind; the other, dark and venomous. His mood could change so quickly. She didn't like to admit it to herself, but there had been times she had been scared of him.

The more she thought about things, she wasn't sure she really knew Ken at all. The way everything had panned out with Ken's move to Bellingham troubled her. Taking him back had been a big decision, one that she had not made lightly. She had done so under the impression that he had followed her there because he so loved her and their son. Ken had called and sent letter after letter, imploring her for another chance. Just one more, because that's all he would need to prove to both of them that he could be the man she needed, the man he really was deep inside. Los Angeles was a bad influence. He wanted to start over on her own turf. A simpler life was just what they both needed. Ken pledged to take an honest job and work hard. He would be present and accountable, fulfilling his duties to his employers, to Kelli and to their son. Never again would he hurt her, frighten her, or lie to her about what he was doing or where he had been.

Kelli had heard these promises many times over, but she couldn't let go of her dream for everything to work out, to finally get her happy ending. Maybe Los Angeles was the problem after all. She knew Ken was impressionable and easily led. He hungered for approval, sometimes from the wrong people. This time, Angelo would be out of the picture. Eventually she had relented, and the first week or so after their reunion had been blissful, and her hopes surged; but pretty soon after, Kelli began to feel that there was something deeply wrong.

He disappeared for long stretches of time and was evasive when questioned about his whereabouts. Kelli found this unsettling, because this time around, he had no known associates in Bellingham. Their intimate life had dwindled down to nothing. Ken told her he just could not feel aroused by a nursing mother. Kelli was hurt, but told Ken she understood—it would pass. Overall though, his unexplained absences and his lack of interest in her did not tally with the passion expressed in his letters. She wasn't really sure why he had come to join her in Bellingham, if it was going to be like this. Kelli's intuition of course was spot on—she and Ryan were not the real reason he had fled Los Angeles.

Kelli had been encouraged by Ken's professional progress in Bellingham—the fact that he had been made supervisor of operations at WSA and been admitted to the sheriff's reserves was impressive. But Ken seemed to spend an inordinate amount of time away from the house "working". Increasingly, he was living a mysterious and secretive life away from her, with who knows whom, doing God knows what. She wondered if he was having an affair. Even if he had no sexual interest in her, he seemed to be unusually libidinous, and had recently turned to masturbating with a small rabbit-fur rug intended for use as a table decoration. One day Kelli found the rug, smeared with dried semen, stuffed in the sofa. Ken told her it was turkey gravy; he had carelessly spilled some when grabbing himself a snack.

Eventually, things had deteriorated enough that the couple were back at square one. Kelli asked Ken to move out. That wasn't long before that strange night when Ken came home pale and sweating; the night Karen Mandic and Diane Wilder were murdered. He had had a strange smell about him.

Kelli's sister Betty was visiting that night. She told the police and Kelli that Ken scared her that evening. He didn't seem like himself. She had felt distinctly uncomfortable around him, and left early as a result.

The concrete evidence against Ken in the murders of Karen and Diane was watertight. That meant that his defense of amnesia and MPD was the only one he had. Ken was either a rapist and murderer, or a lunatic. Neither option was very appealing for a partner.

But Kelli wasn't quite on board with the insanity defense. And that, combined with his troubling behavior after he had moved to Bellingham, implied to her that he had been up to much worse than just having an affair. All the while she read Ken's letters and their promises of love she was nagged by the thought that her partner may well in fact be the worst kind of monster—a man who had knowingly raped and killed many women without conscience.

Chapter 18

Frank Salerno had recently had the pleasure of watching the tape of Ken Bianchi's hypnotic session with Dr. Ralph Allison. He was as unimpressed as ever with Bianchi's acting skills, and even more disenchanted with the performance of the esteemed Dr. Ralph Allison.

—'Do you ever hide in your own head'? What kind of question is that? It's handing the defense to him on a plate, he remarked to Grogan.

—Along with the cutlery and gravy. Have you seen the article?

Grogan referred to the interview with John Watkins in *Time*.

—Yep. Jesus H. Christ. The sanity hearing hasn't even happened yet.

Watkins' very public and premature proclamations about Ken's mental state could be tremendously damaging to the case, and at a minimum were totally unethical and unprofessional.

The detectives were beginning to feel hopeless as they contemplated the prospect that Kenneth Bianchi might actually be going to get away with it. If he was found legally insane, his knowledge of the Los Angeles murders would be useless to them.

They knew that Bianchi had taken courses in psychology back in Rochester, and they had seen the psychology titles that had been in his possession when they sifted through the contents of the house in Bellingham after his arrest. The guy had obviously been studying various means by which he could pull the wool over the eyes of the criminal justice system for years.

When Dudley Varney saw the tape, he remarked that it was quite obvious that Ken was having a ball fooling the shrinks. It was all a game, and it was feeding his ego. It was the classic duper's delight of the sociopath.

But if "Steve" was a character Ken was performing for the benefit of the psychiatrists, at some point—clever as he may be—he was going to trip up.

That moment arrived when, desperate to find the chink in Bianchi's armor, they watched the tape again, this time with very careful and close attention. This time they stopped it at the point where Ken Bianchi mumbled "Steve's" surname.

—Did you get Walker there? I got Walker, said Salerno. Walker, Walker … where have I heard that name…

After talking with Finnegan, Salerno thought they had seen the name "Steve Walker" somewhere amidst the papers that had been retrieved from the Bellingham house after Ken's arrest.

They went through the papers again and there they found what they were looking for. A letter addressed to the registrar of California State University from a "Steven A. Walker". The letter was a request for a blank copy of a dDiploma; one that was complete except for the name of the graduate. The letter was accompanied by transcripts from CSU and a money order. The author of the letter stated that he had lost the original diploma in a fire and wanted to have custom lettering put on the replacement, hence was requesting a blank copy. The registrar had complied with the request, because the letter was stamped "paid".

Salerno and Finnegan decided to pay a visit to CSU at Northridge. There it was confirmed that the transcripts belonged to one Steven Thomas Walker, a psychology graduate from the university. It was looking like the alter "Steve" was in fact a real person: a victim of one of Ken's identity theft scams.

The detectives next sought out Walker himself for an interview. They learned that Walker had responded to an advertisement in the *Los Angeles Times* for positions in a clinic, and he had sent his transcripts as part of the application. He never received a response to his application. The man who posted the advertisement was of course Kenneth Bianchi, posing as a doctor. He had neither the intention nor means of offering anyone a job and merely wanted some legitimate transcripts and a testamur that he could doctor for his own purposes.

Salerno and Finnegan now decided to pursue the trail of Bianchi's deceptions a little further. Kelli had confirmed that, armed with his diploma and transcripts, Ken had rented an office from one Dr. Charles Weingarten out of which he planned to run his "counseling service". The flyers Ken had printed up gave the address at Lankershim, where Jan Sims had had her eerie encounter with Ken and Angelo in the parking lot.

There the detectives were led through to meet with Dr. Weingarten, a perfectly pleasant and professional psychologist who obviously ran an authentic operation.

They showed Weingarten a photograph of Bianchi.

—Do you know this man?

—Oh yes. I rented him an office here. Very affable fellow, seemed very professional...

Weingarten's tone was almost apologetic. Salerno and Finnegan soon understood why. Weingarten had read about Bianchi in the papers, and now knew that he had been charged with murder in Washington, and was a suspect in the Hillside Strangler murders. But at the time he agreed to rent the office out, he'd had no suspicions at all about Bianchi's legitimacy. Ken had described himself as a marriage, family and child guidance counselor, and confidently discussed Gestalt therapy and transactional analysis, amongst other psychology topics.

In fact, Weingarten had been completely taken in, not once, but twice.

When he read about the recent speculations that Kenneth Bianchi suffered MPD in *Time* he believed them, not least because Bianchi had seemed to be such a very pleasant and professional fellow. He was utterly shocked that that same man was now suspected of being a multiple murderer.

—It must have been Ken that I met, not Steve, he remarked to Salerno and Finnegan, who—in different circumstances—might have laughed.

The detectives left their interview with Weingarten angry at Watkins and his stupid article all over again. As for Ken, they were reluctantly impressed by his exploits.

—That sneaky bastard, Salerno said. He fooled that doctor without even breaking a sweat, just like he's fooling the shrinks.

Becoming whoever or whatever suited his purpose might have been second nature to Ken, but he wasn't quite as clever as he thought. After all, he had now made a colossal error giving his cooked-up alter personality the name of a real existing person. So while Ken, tucked away in prison, was ignorantly basking in the glow of his recent wins, Salerno, Finnegan and Grogan comforted themselves with the knowledge that the tide was finally starting to turn.

As "Steve", Ken had now effectively confessed to both the Washington murders and at least some of the Los Angeles killings, describing details that could only have been known to the perpetrators and the police. He had also outed Angelo Buono as his accomplice in the California murders. Taken together with the new eyewitness accounts provided by Markust Camden and Beulah Stofer, the upshot was that there was no doubt that Ken and Angelo were the Hillside Stranglers. This also meant that Ken Bianchi's only hope of salvation now rested upon the insanity defense. So far oblivious to the plans to unmask him, he had painted himself into a corner, leaving himself with no other aces up his sleeve.

This was very bad for Ken. And there was more bad news coming. The psychiatrists appointed by the prosecution to blast apart his insanity defense were about to arrive in Bellingham.

Chapter 19

Based on appearances alone, Kenneth Bianchi might have thought he had little to fear from Martin T. Orne.

Bespectacled and slightly portly, Orne still spoke with the accent of his native Vienna, and seemed every inch the loveable academic eccentric. His credentials however spoke of the fact that the prosecution had upped the ante on their opponents, bringing a heavyweight in on their side.

With a long list of publications and an impressive record of attracting research funds, Orne was head of the Unit for Experimental Psychiatry at the Institute of Pennsylvania Hospital in Philadelphia Hospital and also a professor at the University of Pennsylvania. His field of expertise however was not multiple personality, but hypnosis.

Orne, in fact, was an MPD skeptic. He didn't seriously believe the syndrome existed.

This might have seemed unfairly prejudicial to Bianchi's case, but it really wasn't. The approach, stunning in its simplicity, would be to leave alone the question of Bianchi's MPD diagnosis altogether. All Orne had to do was prove that Bianchi had been faking hypnosis when he summoned Steve into being, and the MPD diagnosis would fall down by itself.

It was Orne's view that some individuals are quite resistant to hypnosis and such individuals, when asked to simulate hypnosis, can deceive even experienced hypnotists. Orne was particularly aware that an individual facing the death penalty on charges of murder had much to gain from such fakery.

The professor's suspicions that Bianchi was faking had been aroused, but by no means confirmed, by the extensive evidence of a history of compulsive lying and identity theft. He reviewed the tapes of the sessions with Watkins and Allison with an open mind, but upon viewing, it took rather little time for him to arrive at the conclusion that Ken had actually never been hypnotized.

Orne decided his first mission was to prove this hypothesis, drawn from his own scientific observations, in a way satisfactory to the legal setting. As it turned out, the task was not particularly difficult.

* * *

Ken probably wasn't quite sure what to expect. All the shrinks had been so pleasant, friendly and helpful. He was forming quite a positive image of the profession. Sure, this guy was working for the other side. But the others he had met weren't as bright as they thought. Psychiatrists didn't seem to be the sharpest bunch. Their intellectual pretensions and blinkered passion for their subject seemed to get them into trouble. Maybe Dr. Orne would be the same.

Orne was as gentle and kind as a lamb, putting Ken at ease with polite enquiries about his welfare. He spoke in a soft, low tone, leaning towards the young "patient". How was he feeling? Had he been eating well, and taking exercise? He needed his strength. He was facing a very tough situation.

But as much as Ken was putting on a performance, so was Orne. It was crucial that he in no way put Ken on the defensive. The guided relaxation technique Orne applied resembled the others Ken had gone through, and Ken immediately and easily "complied". But from there, the game abruptly changed.

Over years of in-depth research and applied study, Orne had developed a number of tests to determine whether a subject was truly hypnotized. The tests differed in a number of different respects, but all were based on the principal that a truly hypnotized subject perceives reality within the limits prescribed by the hypnotist. Information available from a reality outside these limits will not be available to the person while they are hypnotized.

When Ken gave all the signs of being "under", Orne gave him his first hurdle, the so-called "double-hallucination" test.

—Ken, sitting on the chair next you, do you see Dean Brett? If you see Dean, greet him, shake his hand.

Ken enthusiastically complied, shaking hands with the invisible attorney next to him, and even making some polite small talk. Ken was blitzing his exam.

Now for the trick question. The real Dean Brett walked into the room, as pre-arranged by Orne.

—Who's that?

—Hey, Ken exclaimed. It's Dean! How can Dean be in two places at once?

Now he stood up to shake hands with his attorney, for the second time as it were.

Bianchi had failed the test. Had Ken been hypnotized he would not have questioned the hallucinated Dean Brett, the first one sitting in the chair, as the "real" Dean Brett. The appearance of the attorney in the room would not have disturbed his delusion. Ken was trying to show that he had seen the hallucination, when he hadn't.

In the second test, while Ken was apparently hypnotized, Dr. Orne drew an imaginary circle on the back of Ken's hand. He told Ken that he would feel his touch when Dr. Orne placed his hand on Ken's hand outside the circle, but he wouldn't feel anything when touched inside the circle. Dr. Orne instructed Ken to say "yes" when touched outside the circle, and "no" when touched inside the circle. Ken's cleverness outstripped the doctor's when he said "yes" when touched outside, but nothing when touched inside the circle, trying to show Dr. Orne that he had succumbed to the suggestion so completely so as to feel nothing when touched inside the circle.

But this was not how a truly hypnotized subject would behave. A hypnotized person would comply completely with the hypnotist's orders, and say "no" when touched inside the circle, just as instructed.

Dr. Orne congratulated Ken on his cooperativeness and told him he would be back the next day to complete further exploration of his case. Ken should try to make sure he was well rested as the session could be quite tiring. He gave Bianchi no outward sign at all that his opinion based on the preliminary results was that the insanity defense was just another of Ken's scams.

Ken's performance on the tests did not prove in an absolute way that Ken didn't have MPD, but they did show that he had never been hypnotized by Dr. Orne. And if he hadn't, it was pretty clear he had not been hypnotized by Watkins or Allison either—and this was Dr. Orne's very strong opinion from reviewing the tapes.

* * *

"Steve" had on more than one occasion, when speaking with Dr. Allison, firmly denied the existence of any entities besides himself inhabiting the body of Kenneth Bianchi. Orne, having reviewed the tapes of the sessions with Allison, was quite aware of this, and now saw another opportunity to lure Bianchi into his own undoing. Again, this test would not be able to prove definitively that Ken did not suffer MPD, rather, it would focus on his deceit.

When Orne returned for the next part of the experiment, he conducted a conversation with a colleague carefully orchestrated to be heard by Bianchi, even though it didn't appear to be meant for his ears.

Orne and his associate stood on the other side of the room.

—Ken seems to be quite an unusual case, Orne remarked. It's very rare to only have one alter personality. Usually there are three or more.

Bianchi fell into the trap. He had paid careful attention to what Dr. Orne said, and next when Dr. Orne hypnotized Ken, lo and behold, a new, third entity revealed itself. This new alter called himself Billy.

—Okay, Billy, said Orne. What do you know about Ken?

—Ken? I don't know Ken.

—Alright. What is your last name?

—I don't know.

Ken had tripped up on this question before. Now he was more careful.

—What about Steve? Do you know Steve?

—Yeah. He's a bad egg. I stay out of his way. If I stay out of his way, he stays out of mine.

Dr. Orne, while confident Billy was merely Ken's latest invention, was intrigued. The machinations of Bianchi's mind interested him: how would Ken portray this new entity?

—What do you like to do? asked Orne.

—I just want to have fun.

—What kind of fun? Do you have fun like Steve?

—No, you know, he just won't understand that a woman is not just some piece of garbage. He's forever screwing up with women, and instead of just backing off and let it be, he just takes out all his anger and frustration...

The root cause of Steve's troubles with women, according to Billy, was impotence. This was a new one.

—All those girls he killed ... the only way he could get himself off was kill 'em afterwards, or knowing he was gonna kill 'em. And to get it up he had to do stuff like tie them down, restrict them or hold 'em down.

Billy told Orne that Steve's kind of fun, hurting and killing girls, wasn't his bag. His kind of fun was stealing. He styled himself a modern-day Robin Hood.

—The rich are getting richer and the poor are getting poorer. The rich have too much already, so why not take a little from them, even up the score?

Billy took credit for the theft of all the valuables found in Bianchi's Bellingham home, and also fessed up to the scam counseling service in Los Angeles.

This was quite the stroke of genius. If Steve had done the raping and killing, and Billy had done the stealing and identity theft, then Ken was squeaky clean! Poor Ken had never done anything.

As far as Orne could tell, Ken was constructing a neatly compartmentalized scheme of his various personality traits. A little too neat. He was an MPD skeptic, but he knew that those who studied the field always described alters as having full, fleshed out personalities—they were nuanced and multidimensional. In the scheme Ken was constructing, Steve was the violent character who did the raping and killing of the women; Billy was peaceful and non-violent, but devious and deceptive—he was into identity fraud, forgery and theft. Ken was the moral and naïve one—the hapless innocent bystander.

Billy told Orne that he had been created at the same time Steve was, when Ken was around nine or ten. Billy was a liar. He was tasked with creating stories and fabrications that would protect Ken from France's wrath, and later, other authority figures. He was glib, and liked to impress people with tales of his false exploits.

Steve, originally an imaginary friend, had been created to assist Ken to break away from his mother, to encourage him in his independence. Steve's role was to protect Ken by taking on his aggressive impulses, while Billy's job was to defend Ken by lying.

All of this was very interesting, Orne concluded, but hardly convincing. It was overly thought out; it truly reeked of orchestration. And Ken, performing as Billy for Orne, had once again torn the filters off his cigarettes, and then when Ken "re-emerged", expressed surprise at the ashtray full of unfiltered cigarette butts. This too stunk of fakery, because surely by now, having experienced the same several times with the other psychiatrists, Ken would not be surprised that his alters tore his filters off his cigarettes. Ken had probably assumed that Orne had not seen the tapes of the previous sessions.

That was enough for Dr. Orne, and he finalized his report to Judge Kurtz with the unequivocal conclusion that the defendant was malingering.

Chapter 20

The prosecution's strategy wasn't all Dean Brett had to worry about. Not long after Bianchi's interview with Orne, gaping holes began to open in the insanity defense as new evidence was uncovered that contradicted his claims of amnesia for the time of the Washington murders.

It now emerged that Ken, shortly after his arrest, had explored other possible defenses, mainly in the form of alibis to be supplied by friends, family members and other associates. So not only had he been lying about the amnesia, he had been actively trying to pervert the course of justice for some time.

The first sign of trouble was a letter that arrived on Brett's desk from Angie Kinneberg. This was the Bellingham woman who Ken had tried to engage in modeling assignments and told she had a "good body for hooking". When the Bellingham police came asking her questions about Ken she had ratted him out as a "creep" and a "weirdo". Clearly, however, there was something about Ken that she liked, as she had been maintaining an on-off correspondence with him since his arrest, and had even visited him in prison.

In fact, Bianchi had already proposed marriage to Angie, something Kelli Boyd would no doubt have been interested to know. Ken was dangling all kinds of goodies in front of Angie: not only a ring, but money from the book deal he was sure he was going to strike out of his own notoriety.

Ken's sudden largesse owed to the fact that he was trying to persuade Angie to provide an alibi for him and tell the police that he had been with her when the murders occurred.

In his letters to Angie he swore up and down on his innocence, and for good measure loudly vented his disgust at whoever had really raped and killed Karen and Diane.

When I read the autopsy reports I felt so sick. Karen was a nice girl ... I'd love to get my hands on who did this to these girls.

Angie had in fact done just what he asked, and prepared a letter with her signature supplying the false alibi, but she had ultimately lost her nerve. Overcome with guilt, she handed the letter in to Brett's office with a confession attached that it was a fake.

There was another surprise in store with the unannounced arrival of Frances Bianchi at the doorstep of the Bellingham PD.

Mrs. Bianchi had flown to Washington to visit her son in prison, but like Angie, she had been sitting on her own guilty secret she could contain no longer. Ken had written to Frances, enclosing a fake letter supposedly from a former boyfriend of one of the murdered Bellingham girls in which the "author" took full responsibility for the murders. Ken begged his mother to fly to Seattle and post the letter to the Bellingham Police Department. Frances declined to cooperate with this plan; she did however hand the letter in in person, confessing it was all a sham.

—That boy has always been a liar, Frances sobbed. He's lied all his life, even when he didn't have to ... nothing will ever change.

Frances also mentioned something else that didn't come entirely as a shock. She said that Ken had asked her to contact Angelo on his behalf—presumably because earlier efforts to contact him directly had failed.

* * *

Angelo was in no way receptive to any overtures from Ken. Since Ken's arrest in Bellingham he had just been trying to keep his head above water, to keep his business going despite the ugly rumors circulating that he was the Hillside Strangler.

Shamelessly taking the moral high ground, Angelo complained to the police that his rights and privacy were being violated now that he had been publicly declared a suspect in the case in the papers. Now he was receiving threatening letters from strangers!

Dear Greaser Buono, began one missive. *You are a subhuman mutation and your existence is an insult to normal humans. I pray to God somebody kills you.*

What if some nut took it into his head to shoot him, or burn down his shop, and it turned out he'd been innocent all along? How would the pigs feel about that?

They kept coming around, sticking their snouts in his business. He'd cleaned his house from top to bottom to throw the police off the scent, but he couldn't get rid of all the stuff in his garage, because he needed it for his work. Now they were in there poking around with their bags and tweezers. The whole thing was starting to make him very nervous.

And he blamed Kenny. He blamed Kenny for all of it.

Ken had actually made a number of attempts reach out to Angelo since his arrest, contrary to what Angelo told the police. He first penned a letter in which he reminded Angelo of their shared family history and the supposed bonds of loyalty that engendered. But apparently Angelo did not subscribe after all to the adage that blood is thicker than water, because his response was to call Ken at the Whatcom county jail and, using veiled language, threaten to have Kelli and Ryan killed if Ken ratted him out.

Clearly Ken had initially been hopeful that he and his cousin could somehow collaborate to get themselves out of the stink. But the decisive manner in which Angelo shut him down spoke volumes about the latter's feelings on the matter. Angelo didn't trust Ken at all; he was far too crazy and unreliable to be cutting any deals with.

The breakdown of whatever alliance had existed between them could actually be traced back to the events that lead up to Ken's departure from Los Angeles for Bellingham in May 1978.

Angelo was many things: a rapist, a thief, vandal, lout and pederast, but one thing that he wasn't—at least before Kenny arrived in town—was a murderer. This was no reflection on Angelo's ethics or empathy, rather, it was entirely owing to self-interest. He was an established businessman in the city, with a reputation to uphold. Unlike his loser cousin, he actually had a life. Murder seemed a step too far; it was too risky, it potentially threatened everything he had built up over the years.

Until he and Kenny did the first one. They saw how easy it was, and how immensely enjoyable it could be. They got away with it, and then they wanted to do it again. And again.

Things could have worked out fine, in Angelo's view, but for Ken. Ken was naïve, stupid and impulsive. Ken had become the major liability in the whole operation.

Angelo traced the beginning of the downward spiral to the Kimberly Martin murder. It had been Ken's plan to lure her to his own apartment block. That was a bad idea. It had connected them to the victim and brought the cops straight to them. Ken was just lucky that they believed his story when they interviewed him that time.

He was far too excited about following the news of their exploits in the papers. He was obsessed with the Hillside Strangler; he wanted to talk about it all the time! When he'd gone on the ride-along program with the cops, he had asked them to show him the dumping sites. Now that was just stupid. So what could he be saying to other people? The more he blabbed on and on about the strangler to anyone who would listen, the more suspicions would be raised.

When Angelo learned that the cops had been back to interview Ken, not just for a second, but third time, it was the final straw. Angelo concluded that Ken was bringing the heat onto them, and he had to go.

Ken's attitude when he told Angelo about the latest visit from the cops had really rubbed him the wrong way, all ebullient and starry-eyed like some frat boy who had just stolen a keg.

—I fooled 'em again, Ken boasted. Man, those cops are so dumb!

He went on to tell Angelo how they hadn't even joined the dots on the East Garfield address on his license. As far as Angelo was concerned, this was totally the wrong way of looking at things, because the cops probably weren't disclosing all they knew.

—You stupid fuck, said Angelo. You shithead. You need to learn to shut the fuck up. You're gonna get us nailed. You probably already got us nailed.

Shortly after, Kelli left for Bellingham, and when Ken told Angelo he was thinking of chasing after her, Angelo picked up a gun, pointed it at Bianchi's face, and told him he better do just exactly that.

In fact, if he didn't get the hell out of Los Angeles and out of his hair, Ken himself was going to be the next victim.

* * *

Ken continued to write in his prison journal. And yet suddenly, after the visit of Dr. Orne, he seemed to be losing faith in his therapeutic journey.

Now he was wondering what the value of all these visits from the shrinks was after all. Maybe he wasn't really crazy?

I don't envy Dr. Orne his position, wrote Ken, sounding a generous, philosophical tone. *I don't have any real ideas except I don't see how he can reach a definite conclusion. I'm beginning to wonder if the personality I've been told about is not being truthful with me ...*

It seemed Dr. Orne's experiments and line of questioning had made Ken rather nervous indeed. He was now changing tack. Buried in amongst his avowed confusion about his condition was a suggestion that it had been Watkins and Allison who had in fact created the alters and misled Ken.

All of this posturing however was in vain, because anyone that he needed to convince wasn't all that interested in the contents of Ken's journal; certainly not Orne, who was satisfied of his conclusions on the basis of his experiments alone, nor Dr. Saul Faerstein, the second psychiatrist appointed by the prosecution, who now arrived at the Whatcom county jail with even more rain for Bianchi's parade.

Faerstein, who was arguably even less sympathetic than Orne, interviewed Bianchi on 1 June 1979.

When he began to question Ken about the Washington murders, something interesting happened. Without hypnosis or changing personalities, Ken began recalling exact and vivid details about the night in question.

Ken's previous accounts of the night—recalled "as Ken"—had stated that on the evening of the murders he had been scheduled to attend his sheriff's reserves meeting, but he never got there; instead he had "come to" on Willow Road, near the cul-de-sac where the two girls were dumped in Karen's Bobcat. At this point he had noticed a rip in the crotch of his work pants, and had no idea how it had got there.

But now, he remembered what had happened in between.

He had driven over to the Catlow house and met the girls there, he explained to Faerstein, and shown them into the house.

—I had a gun. It's the strangest thing, because I could swear I left my work gun at home in my closet.

Bianchi would return to this point several times; that he was sure his gun was at home.

He had turned the gun on the girls and, with them walking ahead of him, made them go downstairs to the lower level of the house. He tied the girls up with cord and put Diane in the bathroom and Karen in the bedroom on the bed.

—Both girls were untied one at a time and told to take their clothes off, tied back up again. Both girls were sexually assaulted. And the reason they didn't find any trace of that is because a prophylactic was used.

Faerstein noted that Ken referred to his raping the girls in passive voice: "both girls were assaulted". He had summoned the wherewithal to admit the deeds, but he was distancing himself from them.

Ken recalled that the cord used to strangle Karen and Diane was of a very specific type: a strong kind of cord used in hospitals to place patients in traction. It seems likely Ken had stolen this cord, along with the surgical supplies, from the Verdugo Hills hospital in California when he worked there briefly the year prior. He described cutting the cord into equal lengths specifically for the task of strangling the women.

—I led them down to the basement ... following behind with the gun.

He now spoke for the first time about the emotions involved in the actual killing, an intense anger that seemingly could not be sated. But he spoke as if his anger were not quite his own, rather something more akin to a force that seized him. He probably came close to the truth when he explained that this rage was not directed at Karen and Diane themselves, but something larger:

—It was brutal. Brutal because both my hands were just—I mean, shaking and I can see my knuckles growing whiter and whiter. And I had the cord wrapped around my hand, and it was pulling tighter and tighter...

—You were behind them? Faerstein clarified.

—Yeah ... they were face down.

—You were sort of over their bodies behind 'em?

—Right. Yes.

The cord, along with the condoms and Ace bandages, were secreted in a yellow plastic bag stashed under the seat in his truck. The bag was later used to discard the women's personal effects—Karen's purse and some college books.

Faerstein, reflecting on the deliberate and calculated level of planning involved in all this, asked Ken why he had brought the yellow bag.

—All I have is this feeling, you know ... that feeling, it was just second nature to, you know...

Ken trailed off in his characteristic halting style, full of loops, backtracks and apparent confusion, but really designed to obfuscate and distance himself from the very unpalatable facts.

—I just had to get rid of everything, leave nothing behind. Leave the place as I had found it.

Afterwards, Ken hoisted the women's bodies into Karen's Bobcat and drove to the cul-de-sac. It was the effort of lifting the bodies that had caused the rip in his pants. He had then returned to the Catlow house to pick up his truck.

Then there was the matter of Diane's coat and scarf. Ken recalled he had retrieved them from the Catlow house before he left, but they would not fit in the yellow bag with the rest of the girls' possessions. He had put them in the back of his truck and later hid them behind the guard shack at South Terminal.

—I remember being at the guard shack. There was a little spot in there, which had been like the missing link in my thinking of what happened that Friday that I got picked up. I know now that the coat and scarf were put by one of the brick buildings. I think behind some pipes...

—Tell me what you were thinking when you put them there.

—I was just devoid of thought. I can ... I see myself turning, the physical action. I can see myself get out of the truck, reach behind the seat and grab the coat, put the coat behind the pipe and walk back to the compound. What I was thinking ... I don't know.

From Ken's description of the murders, Faerstein extracted two basic points. For one, Ken was perfectly capable of remembering verifiable facts of the murders without invoking Steve.

There were a few loose details—Diane's scarf had in fact been found in Ken's truck, but the coat was indeed located later by the police behind the guard shack at the dock. The autopsy of the bodies showed that the girls had been strangled from behind, just as Bianchi described. And that examination had also failed to show semen traces inside the bodies—the sexual assault by Bianchi was instead deduced from semen traces found on the women's underwear and also menstrual blood on Ken's underwear. This was because Ken had used a condom in raping the women. In all, his new account showed that there was no amnesia for the period of the murder. Ken was confirming details that the police had uncovered in their investigation, but he was remembering them as Ken, not Steve. The psychiatrists working for the defense probably would have said that this was a result of the therapeutic process loosening the boundaries between his various personalities and causing a flood of new memories. Faerstein thought it simply showed that he had been lying all along.

The second point was that, even if an alter called Steve had killed the girls and not Bianchi, the actions of this individual were not congruent with the reckless and impulsive character of the "Steve" that Watkins and Allison had met. There was far too much careful planning and premeditated action involved. Bianchi described how he had flushed each of the used condoms down the toilet, straightened the bed in the bedroom where he had raped Karen Mandic, attempting to make it look like nobody had been there. He had carefully hidden the girl's' possessions in the yellow plastic bag so they could be disposed of, just as he had learned to do when killing girls with Angelo in Los Angeles.

In response to the judge's request for advice on the matter of Bianchi's mental condition and competence to stand trial, Faerstein was very clear that Bianchi did not, and had never suffered from MPD.

This, however, did not mean that he was not a very sick man. Faerstein actually concluded that Ken was riddled with a number of overlapping pathologies, but the list placed Ken in the camp of the malignantly amoral rather than the insane. He included on the report personality disorder with sociopathy, explosiveness and narcissism. Added to that were the unwholesome garnishes of "sexual deviation disorder with features of sexual sadism and violence".

On the matter of Ken's amnesia and his ability to accept culpability for his actions, Faerstein stopped short of stating that Bianchi was purely manipulative. He accepted instead that denial was thoroughly ingrained in his psychological make-up. Ken found it extraordinarily difficult, almost impossible, to face the darker aspect of his nature: the use of psychological defenses of repression and denial since early childhood had manifested in "isolation and splitting of affect, somatization, and what is described by Mr. Bianchi as amnesia".

Faerstein's observations about Bianchi's motivations were perhaps the most interesting part of his report.

The doctor noted that from childhood, Ken had admired police officers and dreamed of working in law enforcement. Faerstein conjectured that he imagined the achievement of this aspiration as some sort of victory over his mother. But he had failed and been rejected over and again in his efforts to realize his ambition of becoming a cop. All of this had made him bitter and resentful; but in his career as a murderer, he showed that he had mastered the science of law enforcement and was better at it than any policeman.

"In the process of achieving his victory over the female authority by killing her surrogates", wrote Faerstein, "he also vanquished the male authority figure by eluding the police, sheriffs and detectives".

Chapter 21

Two weeks had passed since his disastrous interview with Saul Faerstein, and Ken Bianchi hit rock bottom.

His legal situation suddenly looked hopeless; he was trapped, and finally, he saw no way out, having used and abused every last available exit strategy. His predicament was completely out of his hands, and he saw only one way to once again regain control: by taking his own life.

He constructed a crude noose out of torn bed sheets, tied it to the bars of his cell and tried to hang himself. In a truly tragic turn of events, Ken found he couldn't even kill himself. His neck became intolerably sore while he waited for asphyxiation to occur. He got bored and fed up with the whole thing, and gave up, somehow extricating himself from the noose.

If the story sounds a little iffy, that's because there is no absolute proof that it happened. It was reported without external corroboration along these lines by Ken to Ralph Allison, who soon returned to Bellingham out of concern for his "patient" and a desire to follow up revelations from the sessions with Orne.

Ken told Allison that he had tried to kill himself because he was reading things in the papers that his other personalities had been saying in the interviews, that he himself didn't know about. The shock had been "too much". Allison again saw confirmation here of the MPD diagnosis.

Ken was glad the attempt had failed because he soon felt different about his situation. He cut the noose into small pieces and flushed it down the toilet so he wouldn't be tempted to try again. So despite his very clever story about why he had done it, there was no evidence left that Ken had really tried to off himself, except a suicide note cum will which he penned that same evening:

I, Kenneth A. Bianchi, being of sound mind and body, do hereby write this, my last will and testament. To my son Ryan I leave all my worldly goods, as little as that may be, it goes to him with my deepest love. It is profound to me that I have had to experience more confusion and mistrust and insincerity in society, if only the right people had been wise enough to follow through with their responsibilities, during the years of forming me into the mold of adulthood, I wouldn't be where I am now. There's a sadness in misunderstanding, an emptiness like a hollow egg. The egg which can produce life in two ways, one in creation and one in sustenance and not realizing the potential of either.

Ken's egg metaphor is somewhat difficult to follow, but it is clear in this epistolary farewell that, even when Ken seems to be owning some responsibility, he lays the blame somewhere else: in this case roundly at the feet of Frances, the mother goose who had failed to provide appropriate sustenance. To exist is not enough, he seems to say; to exist without growth is to be hollow, and that surely is the destiny of the sociopath. Self-serving or not, Ken did occasionally approach some truth, some profundity, in his thinking about himself.

If Ken really attempted suicide, it seems likely it was that same hollowness that saved him, the sociopath's relentless survival instinct, the only thing that truly animates the blankness. Or, the whole thing had just been another bunch of theatrics.

Either way, it seems the interview with Faerstein had triggered a major crisis. This seems borne out by remarks Ken made to Dr. Allison upon his return to Washington on 28 June. Allison observed that Ken was gaunt and pale, and hadn't been taking exercise or sunshine; he was, by his own account, "quite depressed".

—That Dr Faerstein, Ken said, I just couldn't get him to understand what I'm going through. I tried over and over again to get through to him ... he just doesn't get it!

If Ken was unimpressed with Faerstein's capacity for empathy, he had equally little time for his methods. He wasn't very objective, Ken said dismissively. Ken felt Faerstein had "misapprehended" the fact that Ken didn't actually know what he was doing at the time of the killings.

—Dr. Faerstein thinks that if I have knowledge of things now, I've had that knowledge all along!

That was indeed what Faerstein thought. But Ken at least still had an ally in Dr. Allison. Insofar as it was possible for Ken to have friends, Dr. Ralph

Allison had become his friend; such was their bond that Ken regularly wrote him letters, and Allison had returned to Washington largely out of concern for Ken.

There was, of course, a professional motive as well. Allison had watched the tapes of the sessions with the prosecution psychiatrists, and he was not at all convinced that they had proven Ken did not suffer from MPD. John Watkins had also watched the tapes and shared Allison's view.

It might seem remarkable on first glance that these two were clinging to their diagnosis despite the evidence uncovered and the tests performed by Orne. Allison and Watkins had applied what they believed to be the trusted methods of their discipline and come to the opposite conclusion. They felt, based on their own professional knowledge of hypnosis, that Ken had indeed been hypnotized. They also questioned the emphasis Dr. Orne placed on hypnosis as a test for MPD. They believed Orne's tests proceeded from a faulty understanding of the relationship between hypnosis and multiple personality. Watkins pointed out that multiples, in ordinary life, change personalities as a result of stress. Hypnosis is unnecessary for a diagnosis. Dr. Orne's emphasis on the issue was "academic" and superfluous.

As for Bianchi's now being able to recall details of the murders without hypnosis, that was because due to the therapeutic interventions of Watkins and Allison, the ego boundaries of his various personalities were now disappearing, and they were becoming mutually aware. Allison, in his report to Judge Kurtz, pointed out that by the time of their second meeting in June, Ken's memories of the details of the murders—both in Bellingham and Los Angeles—had been coming into his consciousness in rather large volumes.

"It's been very emotionally difficult for him to handle", he added sympathetically.

Of course, Allison put Ken's suicide attempt down to Ken's despair in realizing his actions as this flood of memory assailed him—not to any despair over the direction the case was now taking.

It should also be said that to watch Orne's tests on a video tape, it might not be quite clear to an outside observer how they worked. Allison didn't really understand the methods being employed, so instead of seeing proof of the fakery, he came away from the viewing thoroughly excited—there was a third personality hiding inside Ken: Billy!

* * *

Allison desperately wanted to meet this new alter for himself. Possibly there was a touch of competitiveness at work. Why had Billy spoken to Orne, and not him? He was feeling left out.

He went into the next session with two main tasks in mind. He wanted to meet this Billy, and find out exactly what he knew and remembered about the crimes. It was also his belief that all MPD patients could, under the right circumstances, access a higher part of their consciousness which Allison referred to as an "Inner Self Helper", or "ISH". The ISH, in theory, knows and remembers everything about the activities of all personalities. It was Allison's opinion that this part of Ken's mind was getting stronger, and would be available to speak with him soon.

Ken had mentioned in his journal certain changes in his habits and preferences since beginning "therapy". He used to dislike coffee, as it turned his stomach, but now he found himself drinking several cups a day. He also found that suddenly warmer room temperatures were comfortable, where previously they had made him sweat. Allison saw these changes of habits many times in MPD patients when the boundaries between alters were loosening and the ISH was getting more powerful. They signified that the conscious personality was accessing the feelings and preferences of other personalities.

It didn't seem plausible to Allison that Ken had researched the fact that such changes were typical of individuals with MPD, and had learned how to fake them. Allison himself had only learned that these were typical signs of MPD after a long period of study. So how did Ken know it?

There was also this dream which Ken recorded, in which Ken described a being that Allison saw as a representation of Ken's Inner Self-Helper.

I met a man, can't remember what he looked like, just that he was a man. He had one hand on my shoulder, it was his left hand. He said with concerned assurance that dealing with my mother wasn't enough, I must break clean.

If Allison could get the ISH to speak, he was confident that many questions about the murders would be resolved. After all, ISH would remember everything that Ken did not. His aim was to reach the part of Ken that was "incapable of lying" and would be able to provide information about what Ken had done, including to his attorney.

Dr. Allison began the new interviews on 28 June. All went swimmingly. Under hypnosis, Billy appeared immediately!

He was a talkative, friendly type, who had some useful clarifications for Dr. Allison.

—Billy, said Dr. Allison, why didn't you come out to meet with me before?

—Because of Steve, said Billy. I was scared of how Steve might react. He might try to hurt Ken.

This explanation seemed good enough for Dr. Allison, but it was a convenient cover for the fact that back then, before he met Dr. Orne, Ken hadn't known he had to have more than two personalities to be a proper MPD patient.

—But you told Dr. Orne you didn't know Ken?

Allison had just noticed a slip Ken made. Billy told Orne he didn't know Ken, but now he had just said that Billy hadn't "come out" in the first sessions with Allison because he was trying to protect Ken.

—I lied to Dr. Orne about that, Billy said helpfully. I do know Ken.

Fair enough, thought Allison. Billy was a liar after all; that was his purpose.

Billy's admission that he knew Ken was useful information for Dr. Allison, because otherwise, Allison couldn't explain why it was that Ken didn't know about the murders he committed, but he did know about the thieving. Allison carefully concluded that unlike Steve, Billy was "co-conscious" with Ken. By this he meant that most of the time, Billy's activities—such as stealing and lying—were part of Ken's awareness, but were felt as compulsions on Ken's part to indulge in things he really didn't want to do, morally speaking. All this explained Ken's attitudes to the lies he had told Kelli. He had been mystified by his own lies!

Why do I lie? He had said. Beats the crackers out of me.

Allison noted for his report that not all personalities had to be unconscious to the main personality; only those that had a marked difference in moral standards. Those "which serve some less ethical needs of the main personality, but not something so drastically different as murder, could remain within the conscious realm."

Dr. Allison's reasoning about the case was twisting, pretzel like, to accommodate the inconsistencies he was seeing.

On the upside, Billy completed a handwriting test for Dr. Allison, in a large, childish scrawl that Dr. Allison was very satisfied to see was markedly different to Ken's normal handwriting.

* * *

When Allison met the ISH, he met an entity that spoke in a low, monotonous tone, unlike Ken, Billy, or Steve. ISH was thoughtful and pensive. He had some interesting information that related to things Steve and Billy had said in previous interviews, things that Allison had been wondering about.

Ken had repeatedly said in his interviews with Orne and Faerstein that he didn't know how, when he had committed the killings of Karen and Diane, he had come to have his work gun with him. He thought it was at home in his closet.

—When Ken was leaving the house to go to his meeting, said ISH, Steve came out and took Ken's gun from the closet. He threw it out the window where he came back and collected it before going to the Catlow's to kill the girls.

Allison scratched his head. All this was getting so confusing. Who was who and went where?

ISH also had a convoluted explanation for why Diane's coat had been stashed behind the pipes at the guard shack at the dock, where it was found after Ken was arrested. Steve had disposed of the coat without Ken's awareness, he said. He had wanted it to be found by the police as this would implicate Ken in the murders. ISH also said that Steve had wanted to play a joke on Angelo, and had hidden the coat there so he could retrieve it later, mail it to Angelo, and tell him where it had come from.

Unfortunately, for every question ISH answered for Allison, he seemed to create a new area of uncertainty. He told Allison that Billy had posed as a psychologist in Los Angeles because he saw it as a good way to pick up girls. But this contradicted Billy's earlier statement to Orne that Billy wasn't really interested in women.

This ISH was supposed to know everything about the actions and motivations of the other personalities, but he sure wasn't explaining all that much. On the other hand, maybe Ken Bianchi was just forgetting his stories and getting them mixed up, as liars often do.

Perhaps the most significant revelation during the interview had occurred right at the beginning, before Allison had even hypnotized Ken or met Billy or ISH. Allison however seemed to have missed its significance.

The information arose from a casual discussion he had with Ken about how he had come to be assigned to work on the case. Dean Brett's first choice for MPD expert for hire had not been Allison, but one Dr. Cornelia Wilbur. Dr. Wilbur was best known as the psychiatrist who had diagnosed and treated the most famous multiple personality patient of all time, Shirley Mason. Mason's case was dramatized in the 1973 Hollywood movie *Sybil.*

—Cornelia is a personal friend, Allison remarked. She wasn't available because she lives too far away, and due to her age doesn't take on many cases anymore. Have you seen the movie?

—With Sally Field! Bianchi exclaimed excitedly.

But then, suddenly he averred; he'd heard of the film, but he hadn't actually seen it; he thought Kelli might have watched it once.

But this was a clue that Ken had indeed seen *Sybil,* a movie that explores in detail the topic of MPD, how it starts, and how a case of MPD looks and behaves. All of this suggested he had a good awareness of the subject probably dating back several years, well before he was charged with the murder of the two women in Washington, and had "studied" how to mimic an MPD patient.

* * *

Dr. Allison was unfazed. The second round of interviews had changed his thinking on aspects of Ken's case, but the MPD diagnosis still stood.

In assembling documents for his final report to Judge Kurtz, he enclosed the results of two diagnostic questionnaires he had had Ken take, the MMPI (Minnesota Multiphasic Personality Inventory) and the CPI (California Psychological Inventory). Ken's result on these tests showed that he scored high on traits that Allison had also found strongly presenting in his previous patients.

Certainly, it is unclear how Ken could have "faked" these results. What was interesting about Ken was that he really was the kind of person, with the kind of background, who tends to end up becoming a dissociative. But that doesn't mean he didn't have knowledge or awareness of his crimes, nor that they were wrong.

Commenting on the MMPI results, Allison stated that they showed Ken to be "a hysterical character" whose major defenses were repression and dissociation. The preferred diagnosis is that associated with multiple personality, namely, "psychoneurosis, hysteria, dissociation reaction, consisting of sudden episodes of unaccustomed behavior, related to hysterical acting out, possibly even with true amnesia."

Allison further commented that Ken's defenses of repression were so severe that he was largely unaware of any unworthy motives in himself or others.

He "tries to defend himself strongly against insight or learning to label his feelings."

Ken suffered from Multiple Personality Syndrome, Allison concluded, but intellectually, he now had an awareness of the physical facts of the murders and was able to contribute this knowledge to his attorney.

He therefore revised his original conclusion after the first set of interviews to state that despite the diagnosis, Bianchi was competent to stand trial and participate in the proceedings.

Chapter 22

Finally, after the better part of a year, the shrinks were done poking and prodding Ken Bianchi. All reporting was submitted to Judge Kurtz and there was nothing more for Ken to do but sit in his cell, and wait for his day in court. He had plenty of time on his hands, having given up writing in his diary; there wasn't much point in that particular activity anymore.

In the end a total of six psychiatrists filed reports with the judge. A further two were included with those reports prepared by Watkins, Allison, Orne and Faerstein; one from Charles Moffett, a Bellingham psychiatrist who had briefly seen Bianchi back in April, and one from Donald Lunde, the doctor who had first seen Bianchi and who had initially been the one to suggest that there might be something profoundly wrong with his mind.

Moffett's report had concluded, rather strangely, that Ken had a valid insanity defense, and was not competent to stand trial, but not because he suffered from MPD. Ken had disclosed to Moffett during their meeting that Steve wanted him dead and had issued commands to him to commit suicide. In Moffett's opinion Steve was not an alter personality, but merely a hallucinatory persecutor, a voice that Ken heard in his head. Ken's pathology in his view was of the psychotic variety:; "probably schizophrenia, undifferentiated type" remarked the report. Moffett stated that Ken intellectually knew right from wrong but psychotic episodes and lack of self-awareness meant he had little control over his violent actions.

Lunde's conclusion was less surprising, given that he had been quite convinced from his first meeting with Bianchi that his personality was so entrenched in repression and denial that his professed amnesia most likely derived from a dissociative condition. He also did not take seriously the possibility that a man of Bianchi's only ordinary level of intelligence could pull off a hoax against the psychiatric profession. He accepted that Bianchi had amnesia for crucial periods of time, and that this hadn't been faked. He based his belief that Bianchi was not malingering in part on the observed history of trance-like episodes in Bianchi's childhood, during which he seemed to lose awareness of his surroundings. He interpreted these as amnesic episodes, and decided that since there was a prior history of amnesia, it was unlikely that Ken was making it up now.

The end result of all this was that there was a split of opinion right down the middle. Watkins and Lunde were of the opinion that Bianchi was a severe dissociative, had amnesia for the time at which the crimes were committed, and was not competent to stand trial. Allison believed the defendant suffered MPD but that he now remembered enough about the activities of his other "other selves" to participate in his own defense. Faerstein and Orne maintained that Bianchi was malingering, did not meet the legal definition of insanity, and was competent; and Moffett had concluded that Bianchi was both insane and incompetent.

What would actually transpire at the insanity hearing on 19 October 1979 was a surprise to almost everyone.

Chapter 23

Never before had so many been packed into the little Whatcom Ccounty court-house. The hearing, one of the most momentous in Bellingham's history, was heavily attended by both local and national press delegates and a goodly portion of curious civilians, including a group of psychology students. The families of Karen Mandic and Diane Wilder were seated in the front rows, as was Kelli Boyd.

But the most noticeable presence was the security. Members of the Special Weapons and Tactics Unit were stationed around the perimeter of the court-room. All attending the hearing had been scanned with metal detectors before being admitted. And then the defendant appeared, wearing a smart but rather tight-fitting pale blue three-piece suit. Under court orders, he was wearing a bulletproof vest under his clothing. All of these preparations were necessitated by Bianchi's actions and the hatred he had inspired in others.

True to form however, Ken did not act the part of the malevolent criminal. He sobbed quietly and intermittently throughout the proceedings like a wounded child. To some the performance was pitiful; to others bizarre. To those present who were skeptical about the claims of insanity, the effort he had taken with his appearance was a mark against him, especially his new, tightly-permed hair. Why had he dressed up for the hearing like he was some kind of celebrity?

Kelli Boyd later said that she hadn't been appraised of Ken's intentions on the day. Bianchi continued to blubber as the damning evidence from the police reports was read out and the charges against him recited.

Judge Kurtz, having reviewed the reports of the psychiatrists, had concluded that Ken Bianchi was competent. Orne's report had been decisive, and Allison's revision of his earlier decision in light of Ken's therapeutic "progress" was also influential. The judge did not make a decision on Ken's state of mind at the time of the crimes; this would be left to a jury to decide. He bound Ken over for trial.

—How do you plead? Judge Kurtz asked.

—Guilty, your Honor.

A gasp rippled through the courtroom.

Through his tears, Ken rounded out his confession:

—Your Honor, I can't find the words to express the sorrow for what I've done. In no way can I take away the pain I have given to others and in no way can I expect forgiveness from anybody.

* * *

Maybe, some onlookers might have concluded, there was some decency and remorse in this morally vacuous individual after all. His blubbering and his sudden decision to change his plea seemed to suggest that there was a beating heart buried in there somewhere. But only ignorance of what had been going on behind the scenes could fuel such an idealistic view of events.

Ken's about-turn was precipitated by developments in Los Angeles, where the case against him was steadily building momentum. In April 1979, Los Angeles Police Chief Daryl F. Gates announced that his people had found enough hard evidence to charge Bianchi with ten of the Hillside murders. Then on 9 May, county District Attorney John Van de Kamp filed a complaint in the Superior Court, initially charging Bianchi with five of these, those with the strongest evidence.

Dean Brett, aware of the developments in California and increasingly pessimistic about the chances of success for his client in the insanity proceedings, had brokered a deal between the Los Angeles and Bellingham authorities to ensure Ken escaped the death penalty in Washington by agreeing to testify against Angelo Buono. The details of the deal were that Bianchi would, in addition to the murder charges in Washington, plead guilty to five charges in Los Angeles. And as long as he testified truthfully against Buono, he would serve his term out in Los Angeles, instead of Walla Walla, Washington, the toughest and most violent prison in the country.

Allegedly, Brett spent many hours the evening prior to the hearing with Bianchi trying to persuade him to withdraw the insanity plea and accept the terms of this agreement. For the longest time Ken insisted there had to be another way; that he was innocent, and it would all be proven in the end. But the evidence against him in the Washington case was watertight. If insanity could not be proven, he was going to die.

Ken finally relented at the last minute.

—I have to take responsibility for what I've done, and I have to do everything I can to get Angelo Buono, Ken told the courtroom, and to devote my life to do everything I possibly can so that nobody hopefully follows in my footsteps.

With Bianchi's change of plea and the deal already in place, Prosecutor McEachran withdrew his request for the death penalty. Judge Kurtz sentenced Ken to two life terms, to run consecutively, without the possibility of parole.

To many, the result seemed intrinsically unjust. Why should Bianchi, who had taken two lives, be himself spared? It felt like the big end of town had steamrolled Bellingham, and deprived them of exacting due punishment.

The DA's office believed that the case against Buono at this time rested almost entirely on Bianchi's testimony, and Judge Kurtz's acceptance of his guilty plea made him a competent witness under the law.

As soon as Bianchi had openly and before the court named Angelo as his accomplice in the Hillside murders, a warrant for Buono's arrest was issued in Los Angeles.

PART FOUR:
THE CONFESSION

Chapter 24

Angelo seemed to know it was coming; it was only a question of when.

He had been getting on with things, putting one foot in front of the other. Such was his commitment to his business that he never went on the run. When the cops arrived at the trim shop on 19 October, within half an hour of the conclusion of the proceedings in Bellingham, he was where he could usually be found, working in his garage. He greeted them with an air of resigned indifference.

Before he was hauled into the Los Angeles county jail, Angelo asked only that a large roll of bills, which he pulled out of his pocket, be given to the owner of the glass shop next door, who would pass it to Tai-Fun Fanny Leung Buono.

—Where's your wallet? asked the arresting officer.

—I ain't got no wallet.

Buono's blasé response to being arrested was in no sense related to a willingness to accept punishment. Rather, he didn't think his imprisonment was likely to be permanent, and spending some time in the can was no big deal to him, since he had done it all before.

Indeed, Buono continued to loudly protest his innocence—at least publicly. Privately was another matter. A fellow prisoner at the Los Angeles county jail, one Steve Barnes, snitched and told the authorities that Buono had told him he had been involved in the Hillside murders and had killed a couple of the girls.

—They were no good, Buono had said. They deserved to die. It had to be done.

It seemed Angelo's confidence derived not from his innocence but from a reasonable opinion that the majority of evidence against him was contained in the rambling confessions of his crazy accomplice.

Nobody would ever take anything Kenny had to say seriously.

—I'm not worried, Angelo had said to Barnes. My cousin's going to go into his little nutbag.

Buono was charged in the Los Angeles Superior Court with 24 felonies, including 10 murders, extortion, conspiracy, sodomy, and pimping and pandering. The case was assigned to Deputy District Attorney Roger Kelly and coprosecutor James Heins. The complaint filed by the DA's office alleged "special circumstances", meaning that the death penalty could be sought if he was convicted.

Thus far, however, Buono's belief in his own inviolability was perhaps not misplaced. The prosecutors were going to have a real fight on their hands. Apart from Ken's say-so, there wasn't a great deal to connect Angelo to the crimes. There were the witness statements from Stofer and Camden, each of which presented their own problems.

But then Detective Bill Williams made an interesting discovery when rifling through a drawer in Angelo's garage: a wallet, the one that he had denied having. Inside, there was a raised holder, the kind used for displaying a police badge. The plastic window still showed an imprint.

And things were about to change with the impending interview of Kenneth Bianchi by the Los Angeles detectives. Ken's ramblings might have been unreliable, but not if they were corroborated by evidence uncovered elsewhere.

Ken had indicated by his confession and naming of Buono in open court that he was willing to testify truthfully against his cousin. Now to see if Ken had the stones to back his word, the Los Angeles detectives travelled to Bellingham to interview Ken in the Whatcom county jail about the Los Angeles murders. Present were all the principal investigators, including Salerno and Grogan, one officer of the Glendale PD and Roger Kelly, the LA county deputy district attorney assigned to the case against Buono.

Roger Kelly was something of a superstar prosecutor. His solid track record for gaining convictions was renowned, but some claimed it wasn't especially owing to any real brilliance on Kelly's part; it was only because he took on easy cases, where there was plenty of hard evidence. The case against Buono wasn't one of those cases, and the detectives were a little apprehensive about Kelly's involvement.

As for Ken Bianchi, skeptical as the detectives were about his credibility as a witness, they hoped that at this point, fighting for his life, he might tell the truth.

They were in for quite a surprise. Not only would they get information vital to achieving a conviction against Angelo, but—for the first time—the whole ugly story of just what had happened to the girls, and why.

Chapter 25

The detectives agreed to conduct the interviews in pairs. The first to go into the room were Williams and Varney, who questioned Ken about Yolanda Washington.

They came out of there thoroughly disheartened. Ken, they said, had given enough patently false information during the interview to throw the whole arrangement into doubt. He'd said that he and Angelo had buried Yolanda under a log, and that the only reason they'd decided to kill her was because they had had sex with her, but didn't feel like paying.

The one useful thing was that Ken had confirmed certain details surrounding the abduction that lined up with their information. He said that a police ruse had been used to entrap Yolanda—a variation on such a ruse had been used on all the victims in fact. Ken had made similar statements when he was performing as "Steve" for the shrinks, but this was the first time he had said it as part of a formal police interview in his lucid "Ken" state.

The detectives had by now spoken with Catherine Lorre, the daughter of Peter Lorre, who identified both Ken and Angelo as the men who had stopped her in the street. She said that she had thought they were police officers. So it seemed that their suspicion that the stranglers were passing themselves off as cops had been correct all along, and Ken was now confirming this for them as part of the official record. It tallied with the imprint of the police badge in Angelo's wallet, the decal that Kelli Boyd had admitted she'd seen on Ken's car, and the statements of the men who had sharehoused briefly with Ken on Corona Drive in 1978 that they had seen a police badge amongst his possessions. Ken explained that the use of a police ruse to lure victims had evolved quite naturally. Angelo had had a police badge for some time and had used it to intimidate prostitutes into doing his bidding.

When he was eventually questioned, Yolanda's pimp told the police that the last time he saw her, she was walking eastbound on Sunset towards Detroit, in the area that Bianchi had identified in the interview as the place where she had been abducted. Finally there was the information provided by Ronald LaMieux, who ran an organ retailer near the corner of Sunset and Detroit. He had contacted the police after Ken's arrest in January 1979, having seen Ken's picture in the papers. He claimed he had seen a man resembling Ken involved in an apparent argument or altercation with a black prostitute that evening of 17 October 1977, near his shop. The man had been waving a badge at her, so LaMieux had assumed it was an arrest for soliciting that was taking place; he had seen the "officer" push Yolanda into the back of a vehicle driven by another man. The cops checked their records and there were no records of vice arrests of prostitutes being made in that area of Sunset that night.

Salerno and Finnegan interviewed Ken about the Judy Miller murder. Salerno was feeling apprehensive, because the testimony of Markust Camden was some of the most important evidence they had connecting Buono to the crime. If Ken's description of the abduction was way off, it might spell a lot of trouble for the case.

He was also more than a little curious about Ken, about how he would act, how he would present himself now that his status as a ruthless murderer was all out in the open. It would be his first meeting with the mercurial Bianchi. He had watched the recording of Ken's session with psychiatrist Donald Lunde, where Ken had talked for some time about Judy Miller. It had been, in fact, the only time Bianchi had shown any emotion in discussing any of the murders. Ken had mentioned that the expression on Judy's face when she realized she was going to die had "greatly upset" him.

—There was this program about executions, Ken had said. They showed these sketches of prisoners strapped to the electric chair, knowing they were about to die ... she [Judy] knew what was coming ... and when I saw the sketches of this guy and his eyes were like this big, because he knew it was going to be the end ... she had that same look in her eyes. When I saw that something clicked in my head. It just left a really bad effect on me...

The sense of emotion in that video however did not cross over into the interview. Salerno and Finnegan found Ken utterly bland and dispassionate during the entire questioning. Perhaps the only way he could identify with the terror of his victims was when he saw it through the eyes of a male prisoner on death row. That, after all, was a situation close to his heart.

Ken's description of the abduction mentioned an important point that told them Camden had definitely seen the same guys. He was sure that Angelo had picked her up near Carney's railroad diner. Ken himself had got in the car later. But there was a problem: Ken insisted they had used his Cadillac that night, where Camden had described a limousine. When Salerno had shown Camden a photo of Ken's Cadillac, he had even been adamant that that wasn't the vehicle.

The mismatch in memory of the events bothered Salerno. He guessed it was possible that Camden had simply mistaken a Cadillac sedan—a large four-door car—with a limo. But that wouldn't wash in a courtroom.

Ken went on to describe how they had driven with Judy manacled in the back of the car to Angelo's. What happened from there set the template for how it went with all the girls. With the exception of Washington, all had been killed at Angelo's house. They fell into a rhythm, a way of doing things, that worked for them. First, the victim would be placed in the brown vinyl chair in Angelo's living room and gagged and blindfolded.

Salerno asked Ken exactly what it was they had used to gag and blindfold Judy.

—The blindfold, Angelo bought this stuff in from his garage ... it was some kind of plastic foam he used in upholstering the cars. We made a blindfold out of that.

Salerno had in his mind at that moment the tiny wisp of fluff that he had removed from Judy's eyelid. He now realized that there was a good chance this material had come from the blindfold. They had yet to match that material, although they had confirmed it did not come from the tarp Koehn left over Judy's body. There was every chance that they would find what they were looking for amongst the various materials in Buono's garage.

—And what happened next?

—Judy ... all the girls, was brought into the spare bedroom. She was assaulted in there.

Ken described how he and Angelo would take turns raping and sodomizing the women. A plastic cellophane bag would be placed over the woman's head with the rope used for asphyxiation enclosed around the bag, wrapped around the woman's neck. They would tighten and loosen the ropes repeatedly during her ordeal; ideally, they would finish the job and strangle her to death at the point of their own climax.

Ken described all this in reasonable detail, but always passively, almost as if it were someone else's body engaged in the actions.

—I'm squatted down, my butt is near her knees, which puts my knees in the area of her chest. While I'm doing this I'm placing the bag over her head...

Ken's habit of describing his crimes using this very distanced language had already been well noted by psychiatrists. They had their own theory about why he did this. Allison had thought that the only way Ken's mind could accept the memories that flooded in once his various "selves" began to integrate was to imagine himself as another person, like someone on a screen, carrying out the acts of rape and murder.

The detectives did not accept this view at all. From their point of view, it was purely an illustration of Ken's gutlessness.

At the same time, the only hint of emotion they got from Ken's circuitous monotone was something well short of shame, or guilt, or remorse. It was more like mild embarrassment, as if he was the kid caught with his hand in the cookie jar.

He knew these actions weren't acceptable in proper society. It was simply awkward for him, to sit here before these men of the law, these police officers, members of a profession he accorded the utmost respect, and tell them how he had desecrated and destroyed innocent women, delighting in their torture, terror and death.

Ken disclosed one final piece of information that was of great use in building the case against Buono on the Miller count. He said that the site at Alta Terrace Drive in La Crescenta where they had dumped Judy's body had been chosen for one quite specific reason.

—It was right outside this house where his ex girlfriend lived ... and he had the idea that she would wake up in the morning and go outside her house and see Judy's body and it would kind of ruin her day. He thought that would be cool.

Salerno knew the ex girlfriend Bianchi referred to was Melinda Hooper. Their interviews with Angelo's associates had revealed that she lived mere meters from where Judy was found. The connection was confirmed when Salerno showed Bianchi a photo of the house at 2248 Alta Terrace Drive. Bianchi confirmed that it was Melinda's house, and Buono had pointed it out as such when they had reconnoitered the dumping site.

Grogan and Varney interviewed Ken regarding Kristina Weckler and Johnson and Cepeda. Again, Bianchi mingled falsehoods with the truth. He at first said that he himself had invited Kristina to the party she was meant to attend the night she died. The detectives knew from their interviews with Kristina's friends that it had been a college party she was supposed to go to.

They put Bianchi's fibbing down to a most distasteful trait they had noted in his character, a narcissism, a desire to appear more important than he really was. The lie was completely unnecessary except in the regard that it made him look like he had more of a personal connection to the victim than he actually did, that they were more than mere acquaintances. They guessed that it had been Bianchi's idea to target Kristina for the simple reason that she had declined a date with Ken, and had injured his pride. Buono didn't know her at all, so the idea had come from Ken.

Bianchi had said before that a police ruse had been used on all the victims, and when they pressed they learned that Ken had gone to her door and shown her his badge, explaining that he had been admitted to the reserves since their prior acquaintance when he lived in the same apartment block. He'd said that he and Angelo had been driving in the area when they saw a man trying to break into her car. She'd accompanied Ken out into the street to investigate and at that point he and Angelo had got her into their vehicle.

They had driven Kristina to Angelo's and once there, as they had done with Judy, they gagged and blindfolded her in the brown vinyl chair. They had moved her to the bedroom where they assaulted her.

He then began to make halting reference to the injection marks the detectives had found on Kristina's arm.

—They said that they ... it didn't really make sense at the time ... they found needle marks on her. There was a variation. Angelo had this idea to kill her a different way.

Grogan and Varney winced at the choice of words. It was almost like he was talking about shopping. Choosing a different brand at the supermarket because it seemed more exciting. And the way he pathetically tried to distance himself from the event, as if it was something he only knew about because he read it in a police report.

—He got this syringe, it had some kind of fluid in it, not sure what it was. Window cleaner maybe ... but it didn't work. And also, I think it was ... she didn't die by strangling. She died by gas asphyxiation.

When the full picture emerged, reading between the lines of Ken's tentative, meandering language, it was beyond horrifying.

After they injected poison into Kristina's arm, she had gone into repeated convulsions, but "she wouldn't die". So they had moved Kristina out to the kitchen. Angelo had disconnected the pipe from the gas stove and they had put a bag over Kristina's head "to make a more complete sealing" so the gas wouldn't escape. They had released gas into the bag until she stopped moving.

—How long did it take?

—Quite a while. Probably like an hour, maybe a little more.

Bianchi's flat speaking voice and passive tone could not conceal the utter sadism and brutality of Kristina's murder. It had been slow, painful, and without a doubt, completely terrifying. Death, when it finally came, would have been a relief.

As unpleasant as it had been, the interview had supplied Grogan and Varney with some very important new facts. When the police had gone through the house at Colorado Street, they had found no fingerprints, but they had noticed something odd in the kitchen, the significance of which had eluded them at the time: the stove's gas line had been disconnected. That physical evidence corroborated Ken's testimony that Kristina had been killed in Buono's house.

Bianchi had also mentioned something that tallied with the coroner's photographs of Kristina's body, something they had entirely missed before. Ken said that the gassing process had left a mark on the left side of her neck, where the pipe had been resting. When Grogan and Varney reviewed the photographs, sure enough, there was a faint line along the flesh where the pipe had left an imprint.

When the detectives questioned Ken about Delores Cepeda and Sonja Johnson, Bianchi's normally slight air of embarrassment seemed to reach peak levels. His language became ever more convoluted and uncertain, positively riddled with ellipses. Ken clearly knew that the imprisonment, rape, torture and murder of two little girls was an unconscionable outrage by society's standards. He just couldn't bring himself to feel it.

Ken's description of Delores' ordeal particularly pained the detectives. She was the second to die. She had asked Ken where her friend was, to which Ken had replied, "you'll be seeing her soon". He then took Dollie into the spare room where Sonja was already lying dead on the bed, and lay Delores down next to her. The face of her dead friend was the last thing Delores saw before she was strangled.

During the interview about Lauren Wagner, Ken's information was equally horrifying, but very useful from a legal point of view. The detectives had suspected from the lesions on Lauren's hands that she had been deliberately burned or electrocuted. She had ultimately died by strangulation, but that was only after repeated efforts to kill her by pumping voltage through her body had failed.

Ken enlightened the officers that again, this had been Angelo's idea. Buono seemed to get a kick out of adding creativity to the proceedings, and he had good technical know-how, plus—due to his workshop being in the back of the house—the various bits and pieces laying around to make it happen.

—He bought this electrical cord in from the shop, and he's … he's torn off the insulation at the end, taped the wires on her hand, and plugged it into the wall. He did it a bunch of times, and she was … she was shaking and moaning, but it didn't work.

Angelo had taped the wires onto Lauren using an adhesive tape he had brought out from his garage. Bianchi clarified that this had occurred with Lauren seated in the brown vinyl chair. The police had removed traces of this adhesive from Lauren's hands and isolated dark brown fibers that had stuck in the glue. They now considered it likely that the fibers may have come from the chair itself. Testing would later confirm this.

The police's suspicions that Lauren had been electrocuted had been kept from the media, both out of respect for Lauren's loved ones and so that any subsequent confession by a suspect could then be conclusively connected to the case. The information Bianchi related about the electrocution could only be known by the detectives and the men who did it.

There was another fact Ken passed on which only he could have known. Lauren had spent the afternoon with her boyfriend before she was abducted, and they had had sex several times. Bianchi reported that Lauren had said, "I'll do whatever you want. It's no problem. I love sex. I enjoy it so much I've been doing it all afternoon with my boyfriend".

Had they not known otherwise, the detectives would have thought Bianchi had made this up—it sounded like the kind of grotesque lie only he could have mustered. But Grogan believed it. It was probably Lauren's attempt to save her own life by demonstrating compliance. It had failed; but since the fact that Lauren had been making love with her boyfriend that afternoon had been kept from the media, the only way Ken could have known that was because he was there.

By the time they got to the last interview, concerning the murder of Cindy Hudspeth, the cops had got enough true information out of Ken to conclusively tie Angelo to at least three of the murders. Kenneth Bianchi had been surprisingly lucid and reasonable, despite minor efforts to derail their inquiry with his habitual lying.

He had proved that where the life at stake was his own, he was quite capable of telling the truth.

As far as the Hudspeth case was concerned, Bianchi would manage to surprise them with just how truthful he could be. Based on the positioning of Cindy's orange Datsun in the gully at Angeles Crest where it was found, the detectives had assumed that the two men had pushed it tail first down the hillside. Ken corrected them. He and Angelo had pushed it into the ravine front first. When the results of forensic analysis of the car's descent down the slope were released, they confirmed that it had plunged front first, and turned once so it landed with the tail pointing downwards.

One thread of Bianchi's testimony bothered them though. They felt that Ken was trying to pin an unfair portion of the blame on Angelo. He had presented the story as if Angelo was the leader and Ken had followed. It had been Angelo's idea to use the gas and the wires. Angelo had decided where to dump the bodies. Angelo had selected most of the victims.

The officers thought Ken had more of a role in things than he was letting on; primarily because prior to Ken's arrival in Los Angeles, Buono, to their knowledge, hadn't been a murderer.

They tried to appeal to Ken's bloated ego. Ken was the smart one, they said; that Angelo barely had two brain cells to rub together. It couldn't have all been him.

But Ken wouldn't relent.

—Don't underestimate Angelo, he said. He only comes off like a dumbo. He's very wise, street wise and smart in a lot of other ways too.

Well, that hadn't gone so well. Ken hadn't caught where they were going and instead it all degenerated into a session of Buono butt kissing. It seemed Ken still looked up to his cousin, even if Angelo didn't give a fig for him.

In the end, the question of who had been the follower and who had been the leader was not one that would ever be satisfactorily resolved in the detective's' minds. Team killers are a rare phenomenon; deviancy is usually a private matter, something an individual feels they cannot share, that is to be savored alone. The conventional thinking is that when killers operate in pairs there is usually a dominant one. But with Bianchi and Buono it wasn't so clear cut.

They concluded that Buono was primarily a sexual sadist; it was Bianchi who had the strong compulsion to kill, and this was borne out by the fact that he had continued to kill when he left Los Angeles for Washington. Angelo, more of a garden-variety asshole, probably would never have killed had he not hooked up with Bianchi.

When the cops probed Bianchi on motive, he made a curious remark: *maybe it's just a matter of the chemistry between two people.*

Ken, ever enamored of Buono, talked about him almost like they were lovers. But the cousins did not have a great deal in common, aside from their prurient misogyny. Their evil chemistry was the admixture of sexual perversion and the drive to annihilate women. Individually they were very dangerous men; together they created a third entity that was incomprehensibly horrific.

Bianchi was unsure of whether the sex or the killing was the primary driver.

—I wondered about this a lot. Was it mainly the thrill of killing, and the sex was a bonus, or was the killing just a necessity afterwards? It could be either. It could be a variation of both those things.

Despite appearances, Ken once said he had devoted a good amount of thought to the question of "why":

—I tried very hard to get a feel for what was going on, the reasons for everything taking place ... basically, the motivation or the emotions being felt. I've always felt a great anger—I mean, a really intense, horrifying, just cut-loose anger ... so one is, was—to get me...

He trailed off, as if he couldn't say the words aloud. He started again on a new point:

—Second, there was a sexual arousal with having sex, knowing that the end product is going to be killing itself. Another is ... this is terrible, and no disrespect to the girls—no witnesses.

Arguably Ken had already paid the ultimate disrespect to the girls by taking their lives; nonetheless there it was, as good an explanation as anyone was going to get. The motive for the rapes was sexual gratification; for the killing, to augment that arousal; and secondly to ensure they didn't get caught.

That casual line, offered almost as an afterthought—*no disrespect to the girls*—chilled the detectives to their marrow. For a few hours of gratification of their lust and sadistic drives, for such prurient and insipid confirmation of their manly superiority, the women's past, present and future, all their memories, their identities, and their lives had been erased, just like that. The sheer mindless selfishness of it was boggling and unintelligible in scope. But, true to form, Bianchi framed this merely as an unfortunate collateral effect of their pragmatism, and tried to imbue his rationalizations with a touch of gentlemanly apology. *No disrespect.*

The cops decided that the speculations about Ken's mental state were a red herring, a distraction. Ironically, it had been easier for the shrinks to believe that Ken suffered from an extremely rare mental disorder than to accept the mundane and ugly truth. These guys were rapists, sadists and haters of women. They pushed their game of debasement and denigration to its final extreme over time, seeing what they could get away with, stepping it up at each level, starting with casual battery and rape with Sabra and Becky, and ending in murder. Murder by increments. It was their discovery of how killing pleasingly enhanced their sport of denigration, and the desire to eliminate witnesses, that took them to that place.

As for the escalation that took place, the cops deduced that the initial killing of Yolanda Washington had had a specific additional motive: revenge. They had wanted to send Deborah Noble, who had sold Buono the dodgy trick list, a message. That murder was probably a kind of test case, to see if they could get away with it, and was carried out by the seat of the pants.

Once they had got away with killing Yolanda, they were compelled to repeat their feat. The pleasure they got from the experience was enhanced by increasing the level of sadism, by employing electrocution or poisoning or whatever other ghastly method they could come up with. It was ramped up again by greater risk taking, by the fear they inspired in the community, when they progressed from killing prostitutes to middle class college students and school girls. Through their shared hatred of women they emboldened one another, egged each other onto the next atrocity.

It probably would never have stopped but for Angelo's slightly greater measure of restraint, even if that only derived from total self-interest.

And even though Salerno and Finnegan had told Ken they thought he was the smarter of the two, truly their money was on Buono, since Ken had been caught within days of committing his first murders alone up in Bellingham.

Chapter 26

Ken, had, so far, had met his obligations under the new agreement, so the detectives now escorted him back to Los Angeles to fulfill the remainder of its terms, testifying against Buono.

Bianchi appeared before the Los Angeles Superior Court on Saturday morning, 20 October 1979.

Yes, I did, he said quietly as Roger Kelly asked him if he killed each of five victims during the six-month killing spree. Judge William B. Keene sentenced Bianchi to five life terms for the murders, one life term for conspiracy and an additional five-year term for sodomy.

Under California law, the six life sentences would run concurrently with the two consecutive life sentences imposed in Washington. Judge Keene, however, remarked in closing that he had fervently wished he had the power to order that the sentences run consecutively.

Ken's recent cooperativeness was not destined to last, however. As soon as he was safely installed in the Los Angeles county jail, troubling signs began to appear that he would not be able to hold up his end of the bargain after all.

The first omen of the difficulties the star witness was going to present for the upcoming trial was a bundle of letters that landed on the desk of prosecutor Roger Kelly. Ken had begun busily writing from his cell, reaching out to "old friends"—really, anyone he thought might listen to him.

Dr. Ralph Allison was firmly in that camp, and Ken had written him a letter claiming he didn't actually remember killing anyone after all. He said that he had only implicated himself in the Bellingham interviews with the detectives because the cops insisted that he was trying to pin too much blame on Angelo. He had only been an observer in some of those murders; Angelo had killed all the girls himself. He knew that they would never believe the real truth, so he had lied. Cleverly, he referred to his habit of using the passive voice in the interviews, using statements such as "they were killed", as meaning, "they were killed by Angelo." He said his only crime was that he had not stopped the killings. He felt bad about that.

Ken sent a total of seven letters to Ralph Allison between October and December 1979. The claims grew ever more outlandish. In a letter dated 10 November 1979, Ken claimed that he was innocent in the Washington murders and said Mandic and Wilder were killed by a Bellingham man named Greg.

There was in fact a man named Greg who lived in the area at the time—he died in a motor crash accident shortly after Bianchi was arrested. Police investigation determined he had an alibi for the time of the murders. It's likely that Bianchi decided this Greg was a convenient scapegoat since he could hardly defend himself against the charges.

Perhaps in a bid to stroke Allison's professional hubris, Ken's new defense on the Bellingham charges revived the whole multiple personality concept.

The letter stated that Ken, as "Steve", and Greg shared an interest in BDSM and kinky sex. Steve and Greg had invited the two women to the Catlow house for a blind date. Steve had gone to the store to buy snacks and drinks, and when he returned, he found Greg in the act of killing the women. When Greg had tried to initiate kinky sex with the women, they had threatened to report him, and Greg—worried about his reputation—panicked.

The letters continued, offering variations of the same story, in which the man called Greg was responsible for the killings. Another version of the story stated it had in fact been Billy, not Steve, who had arranged the liaison with the women. The reason was that Billy wanted to see a variety of women, but Ken would only date Kelli, and didn't approve of Billy's desires. In this iteration of the tale, Billy went to the store and came back to find Greg had hung the women from the rafters. When Billy went into shock, Steve "came out". Steve helped Greg by disposing of the bodies; the letter said that the rest of the police information concerning what had happened after the killings was correct, but that he was not involved in the actual murders.

When Allison made the existence of these letters known to the Los Angeles DA's office, and Roger Kelly confronted Ken about them, Ken claimed amnesia again and insisted on his innocence in all the killings.

If this weren't worrying enough, Ken also supplied a series of ever-changing and contradictory stories to Kelli, his mother, and his old pen pal in Bellingham, Angie Kinneberg. He had returned to his default pattern of denial, and was now seemingly convinced—despite the evidence and his own statements to the police—that somebody, anybody, had to be responsible for the killings. Just not him.

Ken's change of heart could mostly be traced back to the dismissal of five of the Los Angeles murder charges by Deputy DA Roger Kelly. His confessions to the police had been made under threat of the death penalty, and he no longer had to fear that, since he had already been sentenced on all the remaining charges.

Another factor was Kelli and Ryan. Kelli had finally accepted Ken's guilt, and wanted nothing to do with him. The axe finally fell when the cops confirmed her suspicions that Ken's cancer was a sham. They could find no reason for it apart from Ken's wish to take time off work. Or possibly he was trying prevent Kelli from leaving him; or possibly he just got pleasure from tricking her and seeing her upset. Who knew. Either way, that he had so knowingly deceived her and allowed her to be tied up in knots over the possibility of him dying made her sick.

She had begun to date other men, and to plan a future for her child in which the biological father would have no role. Preferably, Ryan would not even know, until he had gained sufficient maturity, who his father was. Ken rightly worried that when Ryan finally learned that his father was a mass murderer, his own son would detest him. He felt compelled to prove his innocence all over. Although now, it was too late.

Lastly, Ken didn't really need a motive to lie and weave crazy tales—it was in his blood; it was what he did best.

In between letters however, Ken sometimes showed a different side, and reverted to the frightened boy who would do whatever the big men told him, even tell the truth. Ken was intimidated by cops. Under heavy guard, the Los Angeles detectives took him out at night to drive around various locations relevant to the Los Angeles case, asking questions, trying to get as much information as they could, anything to build the case. Before them, he could at times be prevailed upon to be honest.

He gave them a memorable tour of the area around the bus shelter near Scientology manor where he and Buono had picked up Jane King all those years ago.

—It just was the usual cruising around Hollywood. Both of us at the same time spotted her at the bus stop. Angelo said, "do you see what I see?", and he smiled at me and I knew he approved, he definitely wanted to take her to his house ... later, back at Angelo's when she realized what was going on, she was getting scared and she said, "let me go, don't hurt me". She was just very, very scared...

During these tours Ken would sometimes get a little wistful as he reminisced about the good old days. The cops found it so disturbing they usually had to share a drink afterwards.

* * *

The preliminary hearings in the case against Buono began in May 1980 and dragged on for an incredible ten months.

The purpose of the hearings was merely to establish whether there was enough evidence to warrant a trial; but that was just the problem. Bianchi had confirmed himself as an accomplished liar time and time again. His testimony was an unmitigated disaster. He would offer two conflicting versions of the same event on any given day. His rapidly changing stories suggested either that he thought the whole thing was a joke, or that he was nuts after all.

Dr. John Watkins had been following the developments in Los Angeles with interest, and he was of the opinion that the latter view was the explanation for Bianchi's uncooperativeness. Watkins held firm to the view that Ken suffered MPD and that his inability to be a truthful witness was a product of the fact that under the strain of his incarceration and the legal developments he had suffered another dissociative break. He would not be able to provide honest testimony, he claimed, because he didn't remember. Watkins wrote to Kelly and offered his services to work with Ken, to help "put him back together" so he could be more productive on the stand. The letters went unanswered by Kelly's office.

Bianchi made a troubling offhand remark one day to coprosecutor James Hein: *give me a script,* he said. *I'll say whatever you want.*

The various issues with the eyewitness statements also put a major dent in any mettle the prosecution were mustering to push forward. Roger Kelly had met with Beulah Stofer and decided she was too old, sick and crazy to have had any idea what she had seen the night Lauren Wagner was abducted. Markust Camden's less than illustrious past and his time in a mental hospital also made him, in Kelly's opinion, virtually useless.

The worst was his response to Jan Simm's account of the attempted abduction of the teenaged girl near Riverside.

—Are you crazy? Kelly bellowed at her. Nobody is going to believe that!

Simms had now tried to relay what she had seen that day to three different men: two detectives and one prosecutor. She was a schoolteacher, and had not yet succumbed to dementia; her cognitive abilities were surely acceptable. And yet none of these men had believed her, even though—as far as she could tell—they were supposed to be the good guys, the ones trying put the Hillside Strangler away. It was beyond perplexing.

The detectives saw Kelly's habit of tearing holes in the eyewitness statements as almost amounting to sabotage.

Everything seemed to be falling apart, and sickened, they contemplated the prospect that maybe Angelo Buono was going to get away with it all. Just like he himself so smugly thought.

There was one bright spot in all this, however. Kathy Vukovitch, a criminalist for the LAPD, had reported preliminary results of testing on the fibers found on Lauren Wagner's wrists and hands. They matched fibers from the carpet in the spare bedroom of Buono's house, where Bianchi had said that he and Angelo had tried to electrocute Lauren, and material found in the crevice of the brown vinyl easy chair.

This was a major win in the eyes of the investigators: hard physical evidence that corroborated Bianchi's testimony during the police interviews in Bellingham. But when Salerno and Grogan brought it to the attention of Hein and Kelly, they were given a lukewarm response. It seems the prosecutors were so focused on Bianchi's terrible performance in the courtroom that they didn't appreciate its significance. Hein and Kelly seemed to be stuck on the idea that the whole case rested on Bianchi's unreliable testimony. Their apparent laziness regarding the case was enough to make the detectives scream in frustration.

Kenneth Bianchi himself wasn't thinking too hard about the Los Angeles case. He was still ruminating about what had gone down back in Washington, and he was angry about it. He wanted those convictions overturned.

With the arrival of some curious letters at his cell, a new opportunity was about to land in his lap.

PART FIVE:
AN ACE IN THE HOLE

Chapter 27

Ken,

You don't know me but I would like to visit you. My name is Ver Lyn. I am a playwright and I am currently writing a fictional play entitled The Mutilated Cutter. The story is about a female mass murderer.

The letter was signed "Veronica Lyn Compton, pen-name Ver Lyn". Enclosed with it was a draft of the author's play.

Ken briefly perused the manuscript, not having much else to do as he whiled away the hours in his cell.

How strange! It seemed to about the murders he had committed with Angelo. But instead of the killings being committed by a man, there was a woman in the lead role. She would strangle her female victims to death and then inject their bodies with semen to confuse the police and make them think she was a guy.

Ken was flattered that someone had thought his life's work worth writing a stage play about; it fed his narcissistic passion for celebrity. But he didn't care at all for the substitution of a female in the role of the male principal character. It seemed like a cheap gimmick, some kind of allusion to feminism. It ruined the effect as far as he was concerned. Ken ignored Ver Lyn's letter.

The mystery author was persistent, however. She kept writing letters to Ken. Eventually she enclosed some photographs of herself, and finally she had his attention. She was a sexy, buxom brunette. Exotic, maybe half Spanish. Ken relented and invited Veronica to come and see him in prison.

* * *

Twenty-four-year-old Veronica Compton had been watching Ken from afar for quite some time. Another young hopeful trying to make it big in Hollywood, she had written stage plays, one of which—*Night Symphony*—had already been performed around town, and was taking method acting classes with the venerable Lee Strasberg. She was invited to all the "in" clubs around town, and had her own office in Beverly Hills and a personal secretary.

She thought she had finally hit on a winning plot for a play when women had started turning up dead by the sides of freeways back in 1977. Horror was the hot ticket in the late seventies, and she was fascinated by the Hillside Strangler. When, in 1979, she saw Ken plastered over the evening news, confessing in court to the murders of the two co-eds in Bellingham, she was strangely touched by his tearful performance.

She had since followed the developments in the Los Angeles case and just knew she had to meet this Ken Bianchi. She got in touch with the Hillside Strangler taskforce on the pretext of wanting to get her hands on the tape of the interviews with the psychiatrists in Bellingham. Lieutenant Henderson suggested she contact Ken directly and gave her his booking number and postal details in prison.

Veronica told herself that her desire to meet Ken was entirely a matter of doing research for her play. To support her own view of what was taking place, she could point to the fact that she was a serious artist. She had read up on criminology and forensics, talked to detectives and doctors and researched serial killers. She kept a file at home with all the news clippings relating to the Hillside Strangler case and the murders and hearing in Washington. Part of being a real writer was doing all the groundwork and getting the "primary sources".

Then there was her financial situation. The appearance of success was superficial, and not reflected on the balance sheet. By the time she met Ken she was living in a trailer out in Carson. She actually really needed the money she hoped the play's success would bring her. She also hoped to cash in on Bianchi's notoriety by interviewing him for an article to be released at the same time as the play.

She firmly believed she was in control of the process. The reality was a bit different. As serious as Veronica might have been about her career, her aura of bohemian privilege concealed a personal condition of chronic disarray.

Like a lot of young people in Hollywood, she was a hopeless cocaine addict and alcoholic. Large quantities of scotch smoothed the edges of her coke benders and helped her sleep afterwards, along with downers such as Quaaludes. She liked PCP occasionally, to keep things interesting.

Drugs and alcohol were not the limit of what troubled Veronica's mind. All the intoxicants, she claimed, helped her forget a past filled with physical and sexual abuse at the hands of a succession of men, first her father and brother and then various others who weren't first-degree relatives but whom she had nonetheless trusted for one reason or another.

Compton's later interviews document a truly astounding background prior to meeting Bianchi. She mentioned being committed to an asylum, being used by a prostitution ring posing as a modeling agency, extensive surgeries for breast and cervical tumors, sidelines as a madam and compulsive Baccarat player in Las Vegas, participation in an international drug smuggling operation, and through it all, countless rapes and beatings.

It's not a stretch to imagine that, with this background and her drug and alcohol addictions, Veronica—like Ken—was a little unhinged. A woman with a past like hers was also well-prepped to fall into the snare of a sociopath. She had known little in her intimate relationships other than degradation and abuse; the Ken Bianchi experience was bound to resonate for her.

She later said that at the time she met Ken she had done and seen a lot, made and lost vast sums of money. But she was exhausted, broken and haunted by a sense of false gains and real losses. She was a Hollywood woman though, and she was driven to be somebody. To her mind that meant money and fame.

Ken was going to be her ticket to the big time.

Chapter 28

—What do you think? Veronica asked excitedly, waiting nervously for Ken's approval.

—It's wonderful! Ken enthused. I liked what you did there, with the female in the role of the murderer...

There is no way of knowing what prompted Ken to revise his opinion of Veronica's play, but it is probable that Ken had reread the script and already been struck by the idea he hoped would secure his freedom.

In fact, Ken was far less interested in Veronica than the central idea of her play. It tied in with a theory about the murders that he already fervently believed, which was that somebody other than himself was responsible. That person might even be a woman. Ultimately though, their gender didn't matter; what was important was that they could be shown to be still active, still out there killing people, while they had the wrong man—Ken—locked up in prison.

—I've done a lot of work on it, Veronica said, a lot of in-depth research.

—Oh, come on, Ken said, smiling. It's very realistic, very true-to-life ... I think you are just like me.

Veronica realized that Ken thought she had written from experience, and was herself a murderer. She hadn't really got in touch with him to do research for her play; she was a serial killer groupie, some crazy bloodthirsty broad who wanted to hook up with a male alpha killer.

Whatever, she thought to herself. She decided to play along. She told Ken she had killed someone, but he was the first person to know. It would have to be their secret. She later explained this by saying that she wanted Ken to think she was like him, so that he would keep talking to her.

Despite this exchange, in which Ken had insinuated that they shared something special because they were cut from the same murderous cloth, Ken insisted that he hadn't actually killed any of the girls in Los Angeles or in Bellingham. They had the wrong guy. He had confessed under duress and he was innocent.

—The cops and the criminal justice system stitched me up ... and now I'll never see my son again.

It was quite astonishing, how Ken could seamlessly go from being one thing to another. He looked so pathetic sitting there in his prison garb, so pale and listless. Despite what she knew about him, this performance tugged on Veronica's heartstrings, just like his repentant blubbery before Judge Kurtz when she saw him on TV. Veronica, after all, had a son of her own, a few years older than Ryan. She could relate to what he must be feeling, being separated from his kid.

* * *

It seemed that each had something the other wanted. Veronica was artistic, educated and well read, her letters peppered with quotes from Shakespeare. Ken told her that he envied her knowledge of literature, and he was probably being honest. He had always coveted higher qualifications and a better position in society than his own aptitudes and diligence could gain him.

Veronica sent Ken books to read, Strindberg and Ibsen, and he wrote her clumsy but not uncreative poems. Eventually they were speaking daily on the phone and exchanging many personal letters and tapes. The interaction had moved well beyond a professional engagement.

She woke early one morning to the droning shriek of the telephone. It was Ken. These early morning calls would become a familiar pattern.

He sounded anxious and distraught.

—It's my mother. I think she's dying.

—My God. What happened?

—Oh, she's been sick for a while. But with my arrest, and going to prison, it's been too much for her. It's tipped her over the edge. I think this is really it now.

Frances, of course, was not sick at all—she was as strong as an ox—but Ken went on and explained to Veronica how she so badly wanted to believe in Ken's innocence, and he wanted her to have some peace of mind before she died. Would Veronica call Frances and tell her that she knew Ken was innocent and that she was going to help him prove it?

—I don't know, Ken…

—Relax, Veronica. Pour yourself a drink.

Ken was hoping that he could use anybody on the outside in his corner—including Frances and Veronica—to influence the press.

As it turned out, Veronica did contact Frances and made several visits to the home she shared with her second husband. They had relocated to California so she could be nearer her son in his time of need.

One evening she and her son even scored an invite to dinner, which they gratefully accepted. Veronica introduced herself as Ken's new girlfriend and told Frances that new evidence would soon come to light that would prove Ken was innocent, and that he would be released in a matter of months.

Ken certainly had his reasons for being so confident he would soon be freed, outlandish though they were, but for now he didn't share them with Veronica. She believed she was falling in love with Ken, and told him that she would be willing to die for him. It seems Ken took this statement quite literally.

He had so much faith in his plan that he called Kelli's sister to ask if she could recommend a good lawyer to look after some real estate matters. He wanted to sell Veronica's trailer and buy a house where they could settle once he was out of prison. As for Kelli herself, Ken had long since stopped calling her and trying to change her mind about him. He was moving on with someone new. The phone call to Linda, Kelli's sister, would ensure she found out about it. Ken probably could have got a referral to a property lawyer from any number of people—he interacted with lawyers now on a regular basis after all—but he wanted to rub Kelli's nose in his new relationship.

Chapter 29

The early steps of the plan were easiest. It might have even been considered fun. Ken warmed Veronica up by giving her the fun part first.

One day he said to her that he had told the cops he had alibis for the times the girls in Los Angeles were killed.

—I told them I was with a woman, a woman in her twenties with dark brown hair, who met me in Universal City. You could be that woman, Veronica.

He needed her help to develop alibis for the times of the Los Angeles murders. He had already confessed to those, but in his mind, that was just a minor stumbling block. He could claim those confessions had been made under police pressure. He believed, with some good reason, that hard evidence could not conclusively be tied to him. The physical descriptions supplied by witnesses were only that: descriptions. All they showed was that a man who *looked* like him had been seen.

He could find his own evidence that would outweigh theirs. Ken and Veronica would document a fictional relationship that had existed between them when the murders were going on, fabricating evidence that they had met up for dates and sex the nights the murders occurred.

He had Veronica go the public library and research newspaper articles for the dates on which the murders happened. He wanted her to find out about the weather conditions, movies that were playing those days, and any major events that were going on. They were creating memories for a love affair that hadn't existed, and those memories had to be as realistic and true to life as possible.

Ken gave her samples of his handwriting and had her practice his signature, so they could fake receipts from their "dates". For these they would bribe bartenders; they also planned to bribe witnesses who would claim that they had been seen together.

The conspiracy was developed along the lines of a play rehearsal. Ken and Veronica imagined the scenes of a real love affair and then recreated them, so they could be remembered effortlessly for the benefit of police. Clothing, locations and dialogue were all included. This was familiar and enjoyable territory for Veronica. She was well and truly in her element. And Ken knew that all this play-acting was stoking the fires of romance in a way that he could get her in exactly the right spot for her to do just exactly what he wanted.

* * *

Veronica surely should have realized at this point that Ken had moved well off the topic of her project, and that she was getting mixed up in an illegal and dangerous scheme. Her explanation for getting involved, or one of them, is that she was losing her mind.

Veronica had been taking more and more cocaine. Whenever Ken met any resistance to his plans, he told her to snort another line, and pretty soon she would be compliant again.

As the days passed it became apparent to her that something was truly wrong with her physically, perhaps mentally. She began suffering from panic attacks. She was jittery, anxious, and sleep was almost impossible to come by. Perhaps naively, she did not relate these problems to her drug use. She claims she didn't understand the possible long-term consequences of cocaine abuse.

Veronica took uppers to get going in the morning, and downers to rest at night. Soon, the downers were having little effect. Now she began to have seizures, see hallucinations, hear voices and was unable to sleep at all.

Hello amphetamine psychosis.

* * *

Veronica began to imagine that she was stalked by a shadowy presence that she called, for lack of a better term, the Boogie Man. He was real, and he was everywhere. Under the car seat, in the closet, under her bed, outside the shower...

Everything was sliding out of control. At work, when she went in, she tried to act like everything was normal. She got into a habit of walking around with earphones and a Walkman, to drown out the voices in her head.

Her friends and associates did not reach out. In fact, they actively avoided her. She was thin and disheveled, with unbrushed hair, wearing the same clothes days in a row. Who was this hobo?

Veronica's world had shrunk. In her madness and isolation there was only Ken, the Boogie Man and herself. She began to imagine that Ken was her only defense against the monster behind the door. If she did what he said, the Boogie Man couldn't get to her.

Ken told her he could help her, but only if he was released from prison. She had to follow his instructions and do exactly what he said.

Ken had been in frequent contact by phone, mail and recorded tapes from the time they met. As the months passed, he stepped it up. He kept tabs on Veronica and made sure he knew where she was and what she was doing. The more he kept her from others, the more he could fill her head with his own thoughts, and the more complete would be his control over her. Now, as the destruction of her mind was accomplished, Veronica began to imagine that Ken, too, was following her. The logical part of her brain, or what remained of it, knew that he was safely locked up in prison. But now suddenly it seemed he was everywhere. She hallucinated she heard his voice on the radio, that he spoke to her through walls from other rooms, and that he knew her every move and thought. Part of the psychotic illness was the illusion of a telepathic bond with him.

Now he implemented the second part of his plan. During visits Ken and Veronica had often discussed ideas for her play. But gradually, fiction was becoming reality. At some point, the boundaries between the play and the real world dissolved. Ken was inviting Veronica to act out her own story. She was becoming the extension of the Hillside Strangler.

Ken had undone her, she would later say. She was his ace in the hole.

He wanted her to fly up to Bellingham and target a woman who fitted his victim profile. She would strangle her, inject her with his semen—just like in her play—to make the authorities think that the man who had killed Karen and Diane was still on the loose. DNA testing hadn't been deployed in forensics, but the semen type, showing that the perpetrator was a non-secretor, would match the semen found on the two co-eds.

—You can do this Veronica, Ken said. You wrote about it.

Bianchi smuggled his semen to her inside a finger cut from a rubber kitchen glove, hidden inside the binding of a book. He even showed her how to strangle a person using his own expertly honed technique, with a homemade rope fashioned from string.

If all this sounded not especially likely to work, the final element was the real coup de grace. Ken wanted Veronica to recruit actors to audition for a play; they would read a script purporting to be a horror film but it would later be spliced to prepare taped confessions. These would be mailed to important individuals connected with the case, along with items ostensibly taken from the victims. Never mind that a real serial killer would be extremely unlikely to go out of his way to bring himself to the attention of the authorities in thisat manner, no matter how narcissistic he was.

Veronica, for whatever reason, agreed to do what Ken asked. Later, she offered various explanations. She claimed Ken said he would snitch on her and have her son removed from her if she didn't do it; that he was going to be transferred to another prison where Buono was able to arrange a hit on him; that the drugs and the psychosis affected her judgment. Ken, she said, charmed, manipulated and terrorized her; at the same time he told her he would look after her and her kid after he was out of jail.

In the end the reasons didn't matter, because on 19 September 1979, she was on a plane bound for Washington, in her usual condition—high as a kite—and about to commit murder, and it was unlikely she was going to get away with it.

Chapter 30

Kim Breed was not Ken's usual victim type. A maintenance worker for the Bellingham Parks and Recreation Department, she had a strong, athletic body, but it would have been hard for Veronica to see that under Kim's clothes and through the haze of drugs. Compton had chosen poorly.

Kim was at the Coconut Grove bar on a Friday night, having a good time, when she met a heavily pregnant woman with bobbed blonde hair. Veronica had altered her appearance with a wig and a pillow stuffed under her dress.

Kim thought she was a little strange—she talked rapidly, leaping from topic to topic with not a great deal of apparent logic. But, if weird, she seemed harmless enough. The booze, and the conversation, was flowing, and within an hour or so they had embarked on a bar crawl around Bellingham that finished up at the Shangri-La, Veronica's hotel.

The women continued their fun in Veronica's room. Kim was slightly astonished to see that her new friend had a stash of drugs and alcohol in there that could incapacitate a small army: pot, Quaaludes, cocaine, wine and a gallon bottle of scotch. Undoubtedly all this was rather unhealthy for a pregnant woman, but Kim was inclined to live and let live. The party went on.

Veronica told Kim she wanted her to help her play a joke on a man. She needed some staged bondage photos. Would she let Veronica tie her up and take some photos of her on the bed?

Kim, at this point quite inebriated, went along. Veronica steeled herself with a shot of scotch and tied Kim's wrists and feet to mimic the characteristic five-point ligature marks found on the Hillside Strangler victims, but did a poor job; the knots were more like shoelace bows, and just as weak. After taking some polaroids of Kim, Veronica went for it, slipping a pre-made noose around Kim's neck and straddling her on the bed. She started pulling.

Kim laughed. What was happening?

At some point it clicked in her mind that Veronica was actually trying to kill her. But she was strong and the ties on her wrists and ankles were weak; she threw Veronica off onto the floor.

Despite their short acquaintance, Kim thought Veronica was a friend; they had a rapport going. So what had just taken place was utterly bizarre. Kim might have thought it was a joke but for the fact that Veronica had kept pulling until she struggled to breathe. She screamed at Veronica, *why did you do that?*

Veronica sobbed and babbled incoherently. She kept saying she was sorry, that he had made her do it. She kept talking about this other person, this man, as if he were behind the whole thing.

Kim didn't understand and she didn't care. The woman was crazy. She grabbed her things, fled through the door and disappeared into the night.

Veronica, dimly aware that she had completely botched the job, started to panic. She knew she had to get back to Los Angeles as soon as possible. She gathered up her things and left the hotel, with the vague plan of somehow getting to the airport.

It wasn't to be; somewhere along the side of a road she puked in some bushes and passed out.

Ken's scheme had been a catastrophic failure. Veronica's drug and alcohol addiction made her more malleable, but there was a trade-off that cancelled out any benefit, since she was too useless to actually execute the plan.

Veronica eventually made it back to LA. She had screwed up, but so far, she hadn't been arrested. She told Ken everything had gone smoothly, that she had strangled a local woman, injected her with his semen and left his hairs on her body; and that she had mailed the tapes, just like he had told her to.

This last item on the checklist Veronica actually had managed. A couple days later Dr. Ralph Allison was perplexed when he received a package containing a woman's bra and a cassette tape. When he listened to the tape—a recording of an unfamiliar male voice taking responsibility for a murder—he knew immediately that its ultimate origin was Ken Bianchi.

Allison didn't have a clue what the package meant, or that it related to an actual murder attempt that had recently taken place in Bellingham. He interpreted it as a hostile act on the part of his former patient in retaliation for Allison's abandoning their therapy together.

A Reverend Richard Bergstrom of Samish Way Baptist Church in Bellingham also received a tape. He was equally confused.

* * *

On 2 October 1979, Veronica was arrested at her trailer by a delegation of officers from Bellingham and the LA Sheriff's Department. After some mental back-and-forth about what had actually taken place, Breed had immediately gone to the cops in Bellingham. The abrasions on her neck and broken blood vessels in her eyes were obvious evidence of a real murder attempt. The tapes—clearly a misguided effort to exonerate Bianchi—and the fact that Veronica was a regular visitor of his in prison, plus her airline bookings, all pointed back to Compton as the logical suspect.

Two letters had also surfaced that implicated her. Veronica had written Mayor Tom Bradley and Governor Jerry Brown insisting on Ken's innocence, and pleading for his release. She was both grandiose and deluded.

Veronica was hauled into Sybil Brand where she was held without bail. As much of a wreck as she already was, she now had to contend with drug withdrawal surrounded by whomat she deemed to be much worse criminals than herself.

When Ken read the papers and realized Veronica had fouled up, he dropped her like a hot rock, ceasing all contact. He had never been interested in her after all; she was merely his tool.

Veronica pondered all this and more while she writhed and sweated in her cell. She was facing life imprisonment; her little romance with Ken had cost her everything, and for naught.

There was an upside though—she finally got clean, not that she had a choice in the matter.

PART SIX:
THE BURNING LAMP

Chapter 31

Veronica had been a disappointment, but she had distracted Ken and filled up the dreary hours of his days, otherwise only occupied with the equally dreary preliminary trial hearings in the case against Angelo. These finally concluded in March 1981 with a decision by Municipal Court Judge H. Randolph Moore that the case should go to trial.

Because Bianchi was represented by the Public Defender's Office, to avoid any conflict of interest, Buono was assigned separate counsel. His defense was now taken over by Gerald Chaleff and co-counsel Katherine Mader. Chaleff, a Harvard Law School Graduate, had come through the Public Defender's Office, but now worked in private practice as a criminal defense expert. Salerno and Grogan had him pegged as the young and hungry upstart, bucking the square system, making sure every long-haired lout and libertarian—even Buono—could get a fair shot under the law.

Mader, a graduate of Davis Law School, was relatively green compared to Chaleff, but was known for her excellent research skills. If anyone could dig up intelligence to undermine the prosecution's case it was she.

A female co-counsel was a win for Angelo. It might dispose a jury more warmly to him, given the nature of the charges, to see that a woman was willing to defend him, and that they could work together. In fact Buono, showing once again that he was much cannier than he appeared, had requested female counsel for that very reason. Buono and Mader actually appeared to get along very well for most of the trial. Their relationship was a puzzle.

The trial was to be the then longest running in American history, taking two years, and more than fifty thousand pages to transcribe. A decision would not be handed down until 1983, more than five years after the first murder was committed. A major factor in all this, once things got underway, was Bianchi's dithering and contradictory testimony.

But another was the defense's first line strategy, which seemed to be to ensure the case was never properly tested by putting forward an endless series of motions thwarting the prosecution's efforts to have it heard, many hinging on minor technicalities of law. Much of the judge's time would be taken up with preparing and delivering rulings on these various motions. The trial proper therefore did not commence until November 1981.

The first defense motion was to set bail for Buono, and Judge Ronald M. George dispensed with this one quickly. The defendant faced serious charges, the murder of ten women in fact, and he would remain in prison while his ultimate fate was decided.

Governor Jerry Brown had appointed Judge George to the Los Angeles Superior Court in 1977. Brown's own politics were thought progressive to the point of parody, as the lyrics to the Dead Kennedy's song *California Uber Alles* made clear: "Your kids will meditate in school". George was considered a strange choice: a moderate conservative. It was probably more accurate to say that he was a centrist, or that he simply wasn't all that interested in maintaining political consistency in his rulings or his opinions in general.

The main influences on his jurisprudence were not ideology, but detailed reflection on the rule of law. He was an independent thinker. A passionate legal researcher, he was never happier than in the many hours spent poring over precedents, statutes and case materials. He was the scholarly kind of judge, not the political kind.

He was also something of a wild card, known for occasionally unpredictable decisions. And nobody, including the detectives gathered in the courtroom—Salerno, Grogan, Finnegan and Varney and all the principal officers who had worked the case—were quite sure what to expect from him.

* * *

Chaleff and Mader had their task in hand: if they couldn't get their client off, they were to get him the best deal they could.

As they got ready to knuckle in, they seemed very confident. Chaleff's statements to the media indicated his firm conviction that the prosecution's case was weak: apart from Bianchi's testimony, he said, there was simply very little evidence of Angelo's involvement.

With their goal in sight, they made their first big move, and immediately moved to have all Buono's non-murder charges—which included pimping, pandering, sodomy, conspiracy to commit extortion, oral copulation, rape and false imprisonment—severed from the ten murder counts.

Those charges, they moved, should be dealt with at a separate trial. The result of this would be that the murder charges could not be considered in light of Angelo's criminal history, and much of the evidence relating to that history would be inadmissible. The request was reasonable in view of precedent, the principal being that juries tended to be swayed to convict on greater charges simply because they had already heard evidence presented for lesser ones. In other words, nobody wanted to excuse Buono for being a rapist, but the layman could well form an opinion that a rapist was more likely to be a murderer, and that wasn't necessarily fair.

Judge George naturally accepted that, and he also knew that failure to grant the motion would risk his decision later being reversed on appeal; but he had already done detailed reading on Angelo's background, and he wasn't at all convinced that Angelo's sexual perversions did not have direct bearing on consideration of the murder counts. In particular, he was thinking of instances of sexual assault where both Bianchi and Buono were present. Evidence of that nature went to the issue of collaboration in their criminal relationship. The testimony of Sabra Hannan and Becky Spears was particularly relevant here, and he wanted that allowed.

George decided to get around his quandary by granting the motion, but with the qualification that "nothing the Court was saying would preclude a proper showing at trial." That is, evidence initially barred might be later admitted, were it for example to be put at issue during defense cross-examination or defense testimony.

The severing of the non-murder charges, forseeable and necessary as it may have been, unfortunately prepared the way for the next move by the defense, which followed a pathetic performance by Kenneth Bianchi on the stand during the first week of July 1981. The quality of his testimony surprised nobody, his favorite answers to any question being "maybe", "probably", "I don't know" and "I can't remember". He said "probably" he had not been present during the murders of the Los Angeles victims at all, and "probably" he had lied about his part in those crimes during the police interrogation in Bellingham. He was retracting his entire confession under oath.

Onlookers speculated about Bianchi's motives. Why must he insist on being so completely useless and obstructive? His punishment had already been decided, he had nothing to gain by this uncooperativeness, in fact it was quite the opposite: had he forgotten that violating the terms of his agreement would send him straight to the infamous Walla Walla, where sodomy and violence would be aplenty, but aimed in the wrong (for him) direction? Perhaps it was the old code of La Famiglia; perhaps he still cared for his cousin, and wanted to protect him, even though Angelo would never have returned the favor.

John Watkins, watching the developments in Los Angeles, continued to insist that Ken's performance on the stand made perfect sense in light of his multiple personality syndrome. Of course he didn't know, of course he couldn't remember! For all intents and purposes, "Ken" was never there.

The reasons ultimately didn't matter. What mattered was that prosecutors Kelly and Heins believed their entire case against Buono rested on Bianchi's testimony.

The following week, with the full backing of District Attorney John Van De Kamp, they delivered a motion to Judge George to dismiss all ten murder counts against Buono. Kelly's motion stated: "the prosecution for murder now pending against Mr. Angelo Buono cannot be predicated on the evidence now in existence and should be dismissed."

The detectives had to hold themselves back from shouting when the motion was read in court.

And yet, this—the worst possible outcome—had not come entirely as a surprise. Not because Kelly was right when he said the case couldn't be won—he wasn't: there was plenty of independent evidence to justify pressing on, even with Bianchi's recalcitrance. The fiber evidence specifically placed two victims in the same place and time with Buono when they died—inside his house. What more independent and convincing evidence could there be?

No, the motion to dismiss was not entirely out of the blue because they had felt it brewing in the background, with Kelly's appalling attitude to the eyewitnesses, his upbraiding Jan Sims and negating her statement out of hand, and with his strange inability to pay attention when they tried to bring hard facts and evidence implicating Buono to his notice.

It was almost as if Kelly and Heins should have been working for the defense. Did they actually think Buono was innocent? What was going on here?

Once the shock dissipated, Salerno and Grogan sunk deep into despair. Should Buono only be convicted on the non-murder charges, he could well be out on the streets again in as little as five years.

—Well, that's that, Salerno said. We're fucked. Over before it's begun.

Five years for the serial rape, torture and murder of innocent girls and women. It was an outrageous possibility, and the idea that the community and criminal justice system could even tolerate it was almost unthinkable—and yet, there it was.

In response to a question from Judge George about the possibility of refiling charges against Buono at a later time, Kelly had told the court that was unlikely unless new evidence came to light, and he "had no reason to believe new evidence [would] come to light". Never mind he already had this evidence in hand. So it was no surprise that Salerno and Grogan's outrage turned to disgust when, on the heels of this, Van de Kamp told the papers that "No one is going to put this case to rest until it is solved."

Such lies!

* * *

Judge George called a week-long adjournment to allow him time to consider the motion and prepare his ruling, but there was little sense of anticipation on the detective's side.

It was a matter of course that the motion would be granted. A prosecutorial motion to dismiss charges was almost never denied, because the prosecution had filed those charges. Such motions were presumed to be made in good faith; what was the point of insisting the prosecution proceed with a case it could not win?

Salerno, Grogan and the others searched their minds for explanations for Kelly's behavior and actions. They seemed mysterious and inappropriate, putting it kindly.

At best they considered it a failure of will, an indifference to the most heinous of crime.

At worst they detected the hidden hand of political influence guiding the case to ruin. Van De Kamp was to run for Attorney General of California the following year. Maybe his office didn't want failure in a high-profile criminal case besmirching their image as they went into that battle. Was that what this was all about? Was Kelly's dick in Van De Kamp's pocket?

* * *

On 21 July, the court reconvened to hear Judge George's ruling. Nobody was expecting a lengthy address; surely the matter would be dispensed with quickly. There would be little to say.

He began by reading out the basic elements of the request contained within the motion, noting that it was made without the likelihood of refiling; that is, should Buono not be tried for the murders, he never would be. But from there his remarks grew curious. He began talking about the court system, about the role and function of its various offices. Those gathered wondered if they had wrongly stumbled into an undergraduate law lecture. Where was all this going?

George's mini lecture of course had a purpose—those gathered needed some reminding about basics of law set out in precedent and authority about the court's duty in responding to a prosecutorial motion to dismiss. The law in fact does not support the automatic granting of such motions. In other words, "the way it's usually been done" wasn't a good enough reason to rubber-stamp the motion. When he built to his point, it became clear that perhaps things were not moving in the direction all were anticipating: "the disposition of charges filed by a prosecution," he stated, "is a judicial function". The decision was ultimately his, not Kelly's or Van de Kamp's.

George then went onto spell out the details of his ruling. He had reviewed the case in detail, and he had concluded that Kelly was simply wrong. The case was winnable. Certainly Bianchi's contradictory testimony posed a formidable challenge, but Kelly's motion had overlooked a great deal of evidence. George listed numerous items of evidence that Kelly's motion had failed to mention, but specifically pointed to the fact that witnesses had identified Buono as the man they had seen abducting victims, and that fibers from the victims' bodies matched materials found on Buono's property. Those points alone justified a vigorous prosecution of the case, in his view.

George's ruling did not speculate on the reasons for the prosecution's failure of nerve, but contained a barely veiled reference to the possibility of impure motives: "[a] prosecutor should give no weight to the personal or political advantages or disadvantages which might be involved or to a desire to enhance his or her record of conviction." He concluded: "[it is] the court's duty to dismiss pending charges only if it is apparent that dismissal would be in furtherance of justice."

The motion was denied.

Once again the detectives had to restrain themselves from making a scene. They maintained a polite silence until they left the courtroom later that afternoon, whereupon they burst out into cheers.

Chapter 32

All along, the progress of the case against the Hillside Stranglers had been hindered by the vicissitudes of human frailty.

So often the players, from police officers to psychiatrists and prosecutors, had been rendered ineffective in their actions by emotional reasoning, arrogance, laziness, the blinkered focus on turf concerns and self-interest, or simply an inability—or disinclination—to look at the wider picture.

There were the cops who thought the lives of prostitutes were worthless, the officials who wanted to look good in front of the media, the shrinks seeking professional recognition, the prosecutors who assumed middle aged women were crazy, and the politicians seeking office. There was stupidity, there was self-aggrandizement, there was sexism and the tyranny of the herd.

Now this enigmatic and unassuming judge had done what nobody could do before: set aside all that, review the case from top to bottom, and make an informed and dispassionate call ... "in the furtherance of justice".

Of course it was far from over, and Judge George's ruling provoked a minor shit storm in the days following. Legal commentators claimed he had improperly assumed the role of a prosecutor. In the main, he declined to comment, merely reiterating the authority for his decision. If it was wrong for a judge to assume the role of a prosecutor, surely it was wrong for a prosecutor to assume the role of a judge, which would have been the effect of granting Kelly's motion. A jury should be permitted to decide Buono's guilt or innocence, not the office of the district attorney.

There was some vindication for George when a memorandum prepared by Roger Kelly to Van de Kamp, outlining reasons for the motion to dismiss, was leaked to the *Los Angeles Times*. The memo made it publicly obvious, after

George's ruling, that the prosecution had not been diligent in reviewing the evidence on which their case rested. The failure to mention the fiber evidence was particularly glaring—and damning. If the memorandum made Kelly look bad, it made Van de Kamp look slightly better, since it now appeared that his backing of the motion was made in good faith. He had simply acted on the recommendations of those he had entrusted with the responsibilities of their office.

When George had handed down the ruling in court, he gave the DA's office the option of regrouping to continue prosecution, or withdrawing from the case. In that event it would be handed over to the Attorney General's office, then held by the Republican George Deukmejian. That, in the end, was exactly what happened. Van de Kamp maintained that, having backed the motion, his office could not now "ethically" proceed.

George Deukmejian had now inherited a case he knew little about, and had to decide—given Van de Kamp's abandonment of it—whether his office could confidently prosecute. He appointed two of his deputies, Roger Boren and Michael Nash, to look at the case with fresh eyes. Paul Tulleners was hired to assist them in the capacity of special investigator.

Boren, Nash and Tulleners spent several days reviewing the case files, the ruling by Judge George, and the communications between Kelly and Van de Kamp. They further conferred with the principal detectives who had worked on the case, including Salerno and Grogan, and quickly came to the conclusion that they had ample grounds for prosecution. They presented their arguments before a panel of expert prosecutors appointed by Deukmejian to advise him on 10 August 1981. This panel unanimously agreed that the case should be prosecuted, and advised Deukmejian accordingly.

A couple of days later, Boren and Nash met with the attorney general.

—You guys go do it, said Deukmejian.

* * *

Judge George granted a two-month continuance, so the new team could prepare their case.

After so much grief dealing with Kelly, the detectives were afraid to allow themselves the luxury of hope when the case was reassigned. Relations between them and the prosecutors had deteriorated to the extent that Detective

Grogan, a man who found it difficult to conceal his feelings at the best of times, refused to speak to Roger Kelly altogether.

Grogan was so disturbed by Kelly's indifference to the case and the legal establishment's protectiveness towards Buono's "rights" that he declared to Salerno that this was it, the proof if ever any were needed that the world had finally gone mad, morality and humanity atrophied to such a degree that it was deemed natural that murder go unpunished. Perhaps these apparently civilized men were not better than Buono, and secretly thought the girls needed to die.

Further, Salerno and Grogan were forever having to massage witnesses back to a condition of cooperativeness after Kelly had berated and intimidated them during their efforts to make statements. The stand-off between the officers and the prosecutors was obviously deleterious for the case. But the difference working with the new team, they were about to learn, was like night and day.

Boren and Nash actually wanted to know what they thought, and what they had in their files. They were incredibly organized, quickly pulling the mountains of evidence into a shape that they could manage, and finding what they needed to make an argument at a moment's notice. These guys were sharp, they were diligent, and they wanted to win.

* * *

At the conclusion of the continuance Boren and Nash were ready and keen to get moving, but straight away the defense hurled in a new spanner. At issue in a decision pending before the California Supreme Court was the status of hypnotically induced evidence. It was expected that following the lead of other states, the California Supreme Court would rule in *People vs Shirley* that the testimony of a hypnotized witness in a criminal case was inadmissible. Chaleff therefore submitted a motion which, if granted, would bar the testimony of the star witness, Kenneth Bianchi, along with that of Beulah Stofer, Ronald LaMieux and several other witnesses.

The result of that would be the collapse of the prosecution's case. They were fucked all over again.

However undesirable the potential result of the ruling, the defense's motion was hardly frivolous. Issues around hypnotically induced evidence had plagued the courts and criminal justice system across the country for some time. Increasingly, the thinking was that such evidence was unreliable and that hypnotized witnesses were open to the planting of suggestion, including by corrupt police officers. Everyone predicted that California would follow the lead of other states and rule against the introduction of hypnotically induced evidence at trial.

But Judge George's ruling on this motion saved the prosecution's case a second time.

Ken's interviews with the shrinks in Bellingham had filled more than fifty hours of videotape and its transcripts multiple ring binders. Judge George studied all these in detail. Watkins, Allison and Orne again provided testimony—this time to the California Court. And Judge George concurred with Martin Orne that Ken had never been hypnotized. So despite his also ruling in favor of the exclusion of hypnotically induced evidence, Ken's testimony was still "in". So was Beulah Stofer's because her asthmatic coughing had prevented the police hypnotizing her. Ronald LaMieux's testimony was excluded.

* * *

Jury selection began on 16 November 1981, and took three and a half months to complete. Such a lengthy process was typical for the California court system, but because this was a case in which the death penalty may apply, it took even longer; the process involved individual voire dire on each prospective juror's view of the death penalty. In a capital case, the prosecution and defense were each allowed 26 peremptory challenges rather than the usual ten.

The final group of twelve and eight alternates were chosen from an initial group of 120 potential jurors, each of which had to survive examination by the prosecution, defense, judge and counsel. The twelve finally chosen were seven women and five men. Two of these were white, and the remainder Afro-American and Hispanic. All but one retiree were working people, the bulk being civil servants or employees of private corporations. These were regular, sturdy folk: educated but not out of touch; reasonably traditional, but not reactionary, in their politics and values.

Now, with the trial beginning in earnest, Boren and Nash spent a good four months presenting evidence about the ten Los Angeles murders. They did not talk too much at this time about Buono and the evidence relating to his guilt; instead they focused on the activities and background of their key witness Kenneth Bianchi.

This was a calculated strategy to ensure those gathered knew the bad news about the star witness before he took the stand. Ken was a liar and could never stick to one version of a story. He was going to make them look bad no matter what. Boren later said that he and Nash had wanted to get that part out of the way.

Ken Bianchi stepped to the stand in June 1982. He was examined by Nash on direct for four weeks.

The first day of his testimony set the tone for the rest. When Nash asked him if he was involved in the ten murders of the women in Los Angeles during 1977 and 1978, he replied, "I don't know". But on that same afternoon, he said that he thought he was involved in those murders with Angelo, but that he could only recall "bits and pieces" of what happened.

At the conclusion of the direct examination, Nash was concerned that the defense might forgo cross-examination and simply say "no further questions". Indeed in this case, it might have been in their interests to do just that. Bianchi, as the star witness, had made the prosecution case look very weak indeed.

But Chaleff's cross-examination of Bianchi had an unintended effect, one that did not work in the defense's favor. The evidence that Ken had provided during his questioning by the Los Angeles detectives in Bellingham could not be admitted at trial, because it had not been given under oath. The prosecutors were deeply unhappy about this, because Bianchi's accounts of the killings in those interviews had elicited important information that could only have been known by the killers and the police, and matched forensic evidence. But Chaleff made the unwise decision to cross-examine Ken on statements made during those interviews, which then meant the evidence was admitted.

As a result, those gathered in the courtroom heard truthful statements Bianchi made that independently lined up with the physical evidence: his account of Kristina Weckler's gas asphyxiation and the attempts to kill her by means of injecting toxic window cleaner into her bloodstream, which was corroborated by the photographs of the marks on her neck and injection sites on her arm; the description of how Lauren Wagner had been bound in the vinyl easy chair and assaulted in the carpeted spare bedroom, which was verified by the fiber evidence; and the mention of a cigar box in which Angelo had kept handcuffs, photographs of which had been submitted into the trial's exhibits.

The court also heard the tape recordings of these interviews, in which they heard a very different Bianchi speaking: someone who used a measured tone, dispassionately laying out facts. It left a powerful impression, one that counteracted the defense's own message that every shred of Bianchi's testimony was directed purely to the goal of getting himself out of trouble and pointing the finger of blame at Buono.

Chaleff's cross-examination was exhaustive, and exhausting. It went on for an incredible four months. By relentlessly tripping Bianchi up on every lie and contradiction the defense would not only show that the main witness for the prosecution was incapable of telling the truth, but were hoping to wear the jury down into a morass of confusion and lethargy.

Salerno and Grogan called it Chaleff's "strategy of beffudlement". It was often successful, but so dull that for much of it the spectator section of the courtroom was almost empty. Court watchers went to watch other trials taking place in the criminal courts building. William Bonin, a killer of young male hitchhikers, was being tried at the end of the corridor on the same floor, and the trial of "Sunset Slayer" Doug Clark, who shot women in the head while they were performing fellatio on him, was taking place directly across the hall. These spectacles were deemed far more entertaining than the Hillside Strangler trial.

One part of Chaleff's presentation however had the court riveted. He showed the tape recording of Ken's confession to the two co-ed killings in Bellingham. Bianchi, weeping on screen and declaring his guilt without any ambivalence, seemed entirely sincere during this performance. But the screening had come immediately after Ken, on the stand, had stated that he never killed the girls in Bellingham and had only pled guilty because his attorney Dean Brett told him to. The message was clear, and the jurors, staring at Bianchi with pursed lips, had definitely received it. If Ken was telling them the sky was blue, they better be seeking a second opinion.

—He's good enough to the point where he can cry when he wants to, said Chaleff. The man's an actor. He can turn it on and off whenever he wants to and however suits his purpose.

But the court also heard, amongst Ken's many lies and prevarications, descriptions of assaults and killings so grisly, so grotesquely degrading, that if there was even a chance Buono was guilty, the jury were going to have a hard time letting him go.

—Angelo didn't have sex with her, Ken said of Lissa Kastin. I did. When she was being strangled, she struggled a bit. I had started the strangulation. Angelo completed it. I assisted.

Angelo apparently declined sex with Kastin because, when they stripped her of her clothing, he was repelled by her unshaven legs, dismissing her as "a dog" not worth a rape. They penetrated her with a beer bottle while she was strangled, slackening the rope several times so she could occasionally take a gulp of air.

Through the narrative a single-minded focus on the women's body parts emerged. As they were disgusted by Kastin's hairy legs, they were delighted by King's shaven pubis—so much so, it inspired them to go after the two pre-teen girls, Delores and Sonja, the next time. In the pursuit of their fantasies, they regarded the reality of the women—their imperfect limbs, not to mention their lives—as an obstacle and an inconvenience.

Bianchi recounted how several of the victims had involuntarily urinated after dying. Buono didn't like this, he was compulsively clean and didn't want the girls ruining his carpets. So they had refined the technique of making the girls go to the bathroom before they killed them. In the case of Judy Miller, this hadn't worked and she had urinated after dying anyway.

Miller was the first victim on which they had applied the technique of suffocation with a bag. Angelo had brought in a Safeway bag from his garage and the men had put it over her head before wrapping the ligature around her neck. They did the same thing with Jane King, who had finally succumbed to suffocation while she was sodomized. She died while Bianchi was climaxing. Before that her total ordeal had gone on for approximately four hours. Cindy Hudspeth, two hours. Delores Cepeda and Sonja Johnson, two whole days.

On and on it went. At one point, under cross-examination by Chaleff, Bianchi clammed up when a group of uniformed school girls entered the courtroom on a civic study excursion. But Chaleff would not allow Bianchi to hide under cover of his disingenuous propriety. If he was tough enough to rape and kill little girls, surely he could weather a little embarrassment. He continued his questioning and insisted Bianchi answer.

Ken's testimony followed an undulating rhythm. At times he was ponderous, omitting words, his logic hard to follow. Then, suddenly, he was "on", fast talking Kenny, giving them a yarn. During afternoon recess, he sat in a vacant jury room accompanied by Boren, Tulleners and Deputy Public Defender Alan Simon. He generally showed no interest in discussing the case. He drank juice, ate cookies and talked about his favorite books and shows.

An ordinary man, a man who liked to read and watch TV. There was no point trying to understand Bianchi. He was beyond comprehension.

Chapter 33

The trial was building momentum when in October 1982, during Bianchi's testimony, the defense once again attempted to have the whole thing aborted.

Chaleff and Mader presented a second motion to dismiss, this time on the basis of "denial of due process". They had belatedly discovered Markust Camden had spent time in a mental facility and that the interview with Frank Salerno, in which he had identified Buono from photographs as the man he had seen abduct Judy Miller, had occurred just a day after his release from the hospital.

The defense stated in their motion that this information had been deliberately withheld from them. Further, they claimed that because the information had also been withheld from the magistrate who issued the search warrant for the house at Colorado Street, all the evidence that had been turned up during that search—including the all-important fiber evidence—should be suppressed.

The submission was graced with the damning title: "motion to dismiss for prosecutorial misconduct".

Mader singled out Salerno for a scorching attack on his integrity. "Honest Frank", she mocked. He had known that Camden was "psychotic" and "delusional" all along. As an aside, the fact that he would choose such a person as witness showed how desperate the prosecution were, how weak their case.

Judge George took the new motion under consideration and the trial continued while he worked on his ruling. After digging around he learned that information pertaining to Camden's stay in the mental facility had been available to the defense, but they just hadn't seen it. They had ten filing cabinets worth of material, some of which was bequeathed from Angelo's previous representatives in the Public Defender's office. The document was there, but they didn't read it.

Early in the new year, 1983, Judge George dismissed the motion. He castigated the defense for their "reckless allegations" and disorganization. They should be sure of their ground before besmirching the reputations of police officers and their colleagues in the legal profession, and throwing the course of justice into chaos. He added that the motion had greatly exaggerated the seriousness of Camden's mental state. The witness was neither delusional nor psychotic, and his stay in the facility was brief and voluntary, not "almost his entire life" as the defense had charged.

Camden, as it was, had taken the stand for the prosecution in the fall of 1982. His testimony corroborated Bianchi's account of the abduction of Judy Miller in most respects, but the sticking point remained the car, which he had always insisted was a Cadillac limousine, not Ken's own blue Cadillac sedan, as Ken had testified.

The investigation had ultimately narrowed the cause of this conflict in Camden and Bianchi's stories to a genuine confusion on Bianchi's part. Because of Buono's trade as an auto-upholsterer, the men had had access to multiple vehicles for use in abducting and dumping their victims. The many different vehicles described by various witnesses had been a confusing element in the investigation. But Frances Bianchi had handed over to Roger Boren an enlightening photograph taken in front of Buono's shop. In it Ken was posing in front of a dark blue Cadillac limousine, like that described by Camden. They therefore surmised that Camden had probably been right after all; Judy had been abducted in that vehicle, not Ken's.

In any case, it was Camden's picking Buono's face from the mugshots that was the more crucial matter in his account, and on cross-examination, Chaleff did everything in his power to highlight Camden's mental debility and thus void the impression left with the jury of that eyewitness identification of Angelo.

Camden lost his patience on the stand when Chaleff refused to accept that he had seen what he claimed to have seen that night outside Carney's railroad diner. Markust had been maligned over and over as a nutcase who had no idea what he was talking about. He was sick of it. California was dragging him through the mill and now all he wanted was to get on with his life. This would be the last favor he would do for them, given the lack of respect with which he had been treated. He told Chaleff that he grasped that it was his job to ask questions, but he really needed to accept what he was saying.

—Why don't you just let it go when somebody says, "yeah, I seen this person"? … my dog had a cold, by God, but she had pups! Apparently something wasn't interrupting her.

Boren and Nash were pleased with Markust's performance under cross. His losing his temper was actually a win for them. He had come across not as someone who was crazy, but someone who—quite reasonably—was discerning a great deal of unnecessary craziness in the courtroom.

* * *

The defense brought in several character witnesses to testify on behalf of Buono. The effect of these was mixed, but ultimately, not very helpful for the defendant.

Several were former girlfriends of Buono's. They had been brought in with the intention of demonstrating that, unlike Bianchi, Angelo was a man who was successful with women. He did not need to chase women; they naturally gravitated to him. The implication was that he didn't need to force a girl into giving him sex and any violence or kinkiness that took place between Buono and the ladies in his life was probably consensual and pleasurable for both sides. To underline their point, they brought in Tonya Dockery, who testified that Angelo had tried to engage her in sodomy but when she had declined, he had accepted it and not pushed the issue.

This testimony, however, since they had chosen to air it in court, now rendered admissible the testimony of Sabra Hannan, Becky Spears and Antoinette Lombardo. It covered the same issue the defense were getting at, but it would otherwise have been barred under the ruling that had severed the non-murder charges and made evidence relating purely to the sexual assaults irrelevant to the case at hand.

Sabra Hannan had in fact been eagerly waiting for an opportunity to take the stand. She had been disappointed when she was initially told that she would likely not get to tell her story, and was delighted when she received the call with news of the about-turn.

As glamorous and perfect-looking as ever, her hair now teased into a massive blonde eighties style bouffant, Sabra related, amongst other painful, frightening and humiliating incidents, how Ken and Angelo had watched on and insisted, under threat of a beating, that she penetrate herself anally with a dildo.

Sabra was living permanently in Phoenix, working as a dental hygienist, and had now married. Antoinette Lombardo was also married, after wasting years of her life on Angelo. Her husband proudly embraced her after she stepped down from the stand at the conclusion of her testimony.

What these women had suffered had not destroyed their ability to love, or to trust. Their triumph showed up Ken and Angelo for the insignificant insects they truly were.

* * *

The defense made some other lapses of judgment as far as witnesses were concerned. One surprise offering was Bianchi's now ex-girlfriend Veronica Compton. She had been convicted for attempted murder in the Washington Superior Court in March 1981 for trying to kill Kim Breed. The news media had picked up her connection with Bianchi, and dubbed her The Copycat Killer. Veronica's defense in that case was that she hadn't really intended to kill Breed, and that the whole fracas had just been a failed publicity stunt to attract attention for her play.

When Prosecutor McEachran asked if she had tried to kill Kim to show that Kenneth Bianchi was innocent of the Washington murders, Veronica denied it.

—I did it with only one intent: as a writer. Not as someone who is trying to supply Mr. Bianchi with an alibi.

Veronica thought the cops would get involved, there would be a big scandal, and then everyone would finally realize it wasn't someone on the loose trying to kill people, it was "just some writer being dumb". Later, by way of further explanation, she said she had dedicated the past several years of her life to becoming famous and was constantly trying to think up new ways to draw attention to herself.

—I am a very good writer, I am very into myself, very much so. I love myself immensely. I am very narcissistic—believe me, I had to have an enormous ego to do what I did.

She likened what she had tried to do in Bellingham to an episode of *Candid Camera*. All she had wanted to do was "blow people's minds".

The jury didn't buy it. The photographs of the abrasions on Kim Breed's neck and the broken blood vessels in her eyes convinced them that Veronica was a would-be killer. They sentenced her to life imprisonment in Gig Harbour.

Now Veronica wanted to get back at Ken, the man who had ruined her life. Her story for the Los Angeles trial was that she and Ken had been involved in a plot to frame Angelo. That was supposed to show, again, how everything Ken did was an effort to get himself out of trouble by making Angelo the guilty party.

A plot against Buono was perhaps one thread of the deranged scheming that had been going on during their relationship, but the plotlines of the conspiracy were impossible to follow. On the stand, Veronica came across as unhinged and overly theatrical, treating the courtroom as her stage rather than a place where evidence was to be evaluated, and once again she failed to convince a jury of anything. She just wasn't as good an actress as she thought she was.

It came out during her testimony that Veronica had been so devastated and enraged by Ken's betrayal that she had started up a relationship with another serial killer in an effort to make him jealous. That man, of all people, was Sunset Slayer Doug Clarke, who was being tried in the courtroom across the hall.

Their romantic correspondence had included pictures of decapitated women's' heads. Veronica later tried to say that her affair with Clarke wasn't real and that she had only responded to the letters he sent her in prison because he had pretended to be a sympathetic stranger, signing his letters with a different name. It didn't matter. The courtroom drew the conclusion that Compton was a loony and a serial killer groupie and as such, her testimony was merely motivated by the fury of a woman scorned.

Boren and Nash were shocked that the defense had put her on the stand. She had offered to testify for them as well, but they had declined. Such was her aura of ludicrousness that they immediately assumed she could only damage their case.

They wondered if things weren't going so well in the defense camp. Perhaps, despite all that was ranged against them, including Bianchi, the tide was turning in their favor.

Chaleff possibly had one final, and very major card to play. Back in August of 1981, the Rochester Police Department and the FBI had got in touch with the taskforce. They were zeroing in on Bianchi as a suspect in the Alphabet Murders back east, still unsolved ten years later. They had been following the developments in Los Angeles, and were stunned when they saw all the similarities in the MO: the strangling by ligature and the dumping of bodies on hillsides and slopes by roads and freeways, with no effort to conceal them.

When Ken's status as a suspect in the Hillside murders was released, they had further been able to verify that Ken had worked as an ice-cream vendor in locations close to where two of the girls' bodies had been found, and that a car similar to his white Dodge had been spotted near abduction and dumping sites.

Now it was looking like Ken might have a whole new fresh set of legal worries to contend with. He might quite literally rot in jail by the time he served out all his sentences.

Chaleff wasn't all that interested in helping the Rochester folk solve their case. If he could show that Ken had been killing girls by himself before he even came to Los Angeles, that would strengthen his argument that Ken had worked alone in the Los Angeles murders too. Ken had killed alone in Rochester, in Los Angeles and again in Bellingham. Ken was the killer, not Angelo. Angelo was just the unlucky scapegoat.

The Rochester murder files had on record the wrist print lifted from one of the victim's necks. Chaleff wanted to know if that wrist print matched Bianchi's.

Chapter 34

The prosecution made a powerful impression on the jury when all twelve jurors were taken on tours of key locations around Los Angeles. The jurors visited the Tamarind Apartments, 809 East Garfield, Carney's Railroad Diner, Alta Terrace Drive and all the other abduction and dumping spots. They also went to the site of Buono's Colorado Street residence and shop. This visit was less enlightening, because the house and garage no longer existed; it had mysteriously been razed to the ground some months after Buono's arrest. There was suspicion that Buono had arranged with the owner of the glass shop next door to have the structures demolished, so that no more incriminating evidence could be found at the site. But nothing could be proven.

Then, in December 1982, under cover of darkness, Judge George convened the trial at Landa Street, the "cow patch" where the bodies of Delores Cepeda and Sonja Johnson had been dumped. There was something very special about this mysterious little spot—something apart from the fact that Angelo had taken his wives and kids there for iced tea and sandwiches.

Dudley Varney gathered the jurors at the top of the slope that rolled down to the Elysian Valley. He pointed to the spot where the bodies of Dollie and Sonja had been found, where Armando Guerrero had fossicked in the garbage and spied what he assumed to be two mannequins. Now Varney told them to look up into the night sky, to the north. There a police helicopter was flying, its spotlight illuminating an area of the Los Feliz offramp of the Golden State Freeway. That, said Varney, is where Jane King was found. The helicopter flew over them, towards higher ground behind the patch, and threw its light onto Alvarado Street, where Kimberly Martin's body was discovered. On the other side of the valley, Wagner and Weckler. By following the spotlight with their eyes, eventually the jurors could identify almost all the dumping locations; additionally, they could see the Colorado Street location where Buono's house had stood, roughly right in the center of all the other sites, as well as Jennifer Buono's house. And they were all visible from Landa Street.

This elaborate excursion was Boren and Nash's idea, and had gone ahead despite noisy objections from the defense. The prosecutors were satisfied however that it had been tremendously worthwhile. It illustrated that the network of body sites mapped Buono's personal world. These were not places of particular significance to Ken Bianchi, Rochester born and bred, the man the defense were arguing had committed the murders alone. Angelo intimately knew and loved the Glendale area and its surrounding hills. Perversely he had demonstrated his love by littering it with sacrificial victims.

Angelo himself had the right to attend these jury views but had refused. He would have had to appear in front of the jurors in his shackles, which would be both prejudicial and humiliating; but that possibly wasn't the sole or even the most important reason he hadn't joined.

Anyone observing could see that Angelo was losing interest in his case, possibly sensing all was lost. He had remained impassive throughout the proceedings, often staring at the floor. At times he appeared to be asleep. He had lost a significant amount of weight, and his once black hair was now almost completely grey.

During Bianchi's testimony, he remained unmoved, refusing to make eye contact with his cousin and accomplice. His contempt for Kenny was nonetheless palpable, seeming to radiate from his still, slack body like a dark aura.

In October Angelo gave a telephone interview to the KNXT network. He told the reporter he had no idea what was going on in the courtroom. He'd never been in court before. What the hell were they all talking about?

—I'm getting gassed in there, man. The State of California railroaded my ass. I'm all for an eye for an eye. If I killed somebody I'll go to the chamber, no problem. But I never killed nobody.

Meanwhile, while accompanying Tulleners on some investigative work, Boren spoke with a former associate of Buono's, a small-time crook living in Eagle Rock. The man mentioned a conversation he had with Angelo once.

—You know what he said to me? He said, "you never know what a guy gets up to at night".

* * *

Angelo's discontent came to a head one day when he refused to leave his cell and come into court. He'd heard enough.

As a supporting aside, he mentioned that the seats in the courtroom were very uncomfortable and hurt his back. Judge George, not overly sympathetic to Angelo's complaints about the perfectly adequate courtroom chairs, reminded him he was required by law to attend his own trial.

Then there were rumblings that Angelo had been fighting with Chaleff and Mader. Angelo was not grateful for all they had done for him. Whatever anyone privately thought of Gerald and Kathy, of their decision to spend their lives helping society's homicidal scumbags evade punishment, they had made valiant and tireless efforts on behalf of their client.

After such a promising start, all was evidently not well in camp Buono.

Surely, it did not look good for Angelo that family members, and those who should have been friends and allies, had come in to testify for his opponents. Among those witnesses were his sons, Peter and Anthony. They stated for the prosecution that in Angelo's glory days they had accompanied him on "joyrides" around Hollywood, during which he had delighted in playing a favorite practical joke on the prostitutes along Sunset: pretending to solicit them for an encounter and then tricking them (and terrifying them) by producing a police badge.

Angelo's old friend and flatmate, Artie Ford, also took the stand. Ford told the court that he had given Buono a police badge that he found in a bar after a vice officer dropped it during a raid. He stated that he had seen Buono using the badge to harass a prostitute out the front of an organ store near the intersection of Sunset and La Brea.

The significance of that statement would elude the jury, as they had only heard the testimony of Ken Bianchi in relation to the abduction of Yolanda Washington, and Ronald LaMieux's testimony had been barred: but the organ store sounded suspiciously like LaMieux's, and it was possible that the "harassment" Artie witnessed was the prelude to the abduction of Washington.

There was another surprise: Artie said of his connection to Buono, "I loved him".

This raised the admittedly auxiliary question of whether Angelo was bisexual and had engaged in relationships with men as well as women. Nobody would ever know for sure, but it seemed that, for whatever mysterious reason, few were immune to his magnetic charms.

Chapter 35

In August of 1983, the prosecutors were getting ready to rest their case. They had called nearly 250 witnesses already, but in keeping with good practice they had kept their best for last.

The final three to take the stand were Cheryl Burke, Catherine Lorre and Jan Sims, all of whom could offer a direct eyewitness sighting of Buono in connection with the case. Beulah Stofer, the other key eyewitness aside from Camden, had also testified but Boren and Nash scheduled her earlier, due to the fact that her poor vision had made her statement much weaker.

Of the three, only Jan Sims had witnessed an actual abduction attempt, but the testimony of Lorre and Burke linked to the case in other ways that were important. Burke had been in the Hollywood library the night that Kimberly Martin was murdered, and testified to Bianchi and Buono's presence there that same evening. This was significant because the fateful phone call to the agency that had led to Ms. Martin's murder had been made that night from the library.

Ms. Burke's testimony took an interesting turn while she was on the stand. While responding to Nash's questions she suddenly froze and was momentarily mute. It was the first time she had laid eyes on Angelo since that evening, and she was terrified. When she gathered her words again she indicated that "that man" was the one who had stalked her in the stacks that evening. Her words to describe Buono: "utterly predatory".

The defense tried to impugn Cathy Lorre's testimony by pointing to a minor inconsistency in her story. She had told the detectives in her original statement that she had been returning from a class at medical school when the encounter with Bianchi and Buono had occurred. She later remembered that this wasn't correct. The defense leapt on this as a sign that her whole statement was suspect; if she could lie about or misremember one aspect of the story then why should they believe the rest of it? But the account she had given of that day when Bianchi and Buono had tried to pick her up but then, mysteriously, let her go at the last minute exactly lined up with Bianchi's account, and it was this, rather than the small details, that left an impression on the jury.

Jan Simms had demonstrated infinite patience in her dealings with cops and prosecutors, telling them over and over again what she had seen that February day in 1978, despite their refusal to listen. Now she gave her story all over again, this time on the stand as the prosecution's final witness. She verified that Buono was the man she had seen trying to drag the teenaged girl into a car, and that Bianchi had been in the driver's seat. She described the car as an Excalibur or "Excalibur-like" sports car.

This vehicle had been the source of some consternation to Tulleners, who had been unable to verify that such a car had ever been registered to Buono by means of vehicle record checks in California and Nevada. Later he, Boren and Nash discovered that Buono had built the vehicle himself; it was a "kit" car resembling an Excalibur, and because it was a DIY, Buono had never had it registered. However, they were able to obtain statements from associates of Angelo's that they had seen this car parked at his garage on a number of occasions.

Boren and Nash felt they had built towards a strong finish. The defense rested on 2 August, and it was clear to them that, even with all that stood against them in the beginning, they would probably be able to convict Buono on at least some of the counts. They were feeling most confident about the cases for which they had physical evidence: Miller, Wagner and Weckler.

But long experience had taught them to never assume anything about which way a jury would go, so during the recess set aside for preparation of final arguments, they left nothing to chance.

* * *

October came, and it was Angelo Buono's forty-ninth birthday; the second he had spent in the criminal courts building. Katherine Mader arranged for him to have a birthday cake, as she had done the year before. At times during the trial she had fussed and fawned over him, draping an arm around his bony shoulder, whispering to him softly like a he was a grisly baby in need of comfort, but now Angelo seemed to have tired of these theatrics, along with everything else.

If he had hoped that this would be the last birthday he would spend in custody, those hopes were fading. When Chaleff made his closing arguments, it became clear that they would have been good ones for the trial they thought they were going to have; not the one that had, rather unexpectedly, transpired in the end. The premise of the defense's narrative was that Bianchi had committed the murders by himself—or possibly, with another accomplice, but not Angelo. Ken had fingered Angelo merely so he could broker the deal that had enabled him to evade the death penalty. That behavior was all of a piece with Bianchi's history as a liar and conman par excellence. And because Bianchi was so dishonest, his statements about Buono's involvement could never be trusted.

This argument would have been great if all the prosecution had to buttress their own line that Bianchi and Buono had committed the murders together was Bianchi's own testimony. As it was, Chaleff's withering attack on Bianchi's credibility, as reasonable as it was, only ripped out a small chunk of the prosecution's case. They had, in the end, presented a formidable amount of corroborating and independent evidence. The defense's arguments had done little to undermine that evidence.

To drive this home, Nash had prepared a visual aid, a large chart which he affixed to the courtroom wall. On it he listed a series of dot points, each a summary of evidence that pointed to Buono. On the list Nash included the geographical links to Buono represented by the abduction and dumping sites; eyewitness statements linking Buono to abduction events; Buono's personal relationship and history with Bianchi; evidence he was in possession of police paraphernalia and had used police ruses in harassing prostitutes and in the attempted abduction of Cathy Lorre; evidence that there were two killers involved, not one—as indicated by the placement of bodies and the dumping of Cindy Hudspeth's Orange Datsun at Angeles Crest; evidence of prior contact between Buono and two of the victims (Hudspeth and Washington); evidence suggesting consciousness of guilt (Angelo had denied owning a police badge and had hidden his wallet, with a window for a police badge inside, from the police, and had lied to Grogan and Finnegan about his history with Bianchi when first interviewed); and lastly, the crucial fiber evidence.

None of the items listed had come from Bianchi's unreliable testimony. Nonetheless, they tallied with important parts of that testimony. To make that point, Nash then reiterated key statements Ken had made to the Los Angeles detectives during the interview in Bellingham, statements which had turned out to corroborate the independent evidence listed on the chart.

Boren rounded out this presentation by underlining that regardless of Bianchi's eyewitness testimony, their case had essentially rested on a wealth of circumstantial evidence which showed undeniable proof of a "homicidal partnership" between Bianchi and Buono that revealed itself in links between the two men, the murders, the body dump locations and Angelo's residence. And during their presentation of police evidence, they had shown conclusively that these killings had been committed by two individuals, not one. The prosecution concluded by going through the evidence connecting Buono to each individual count.

Mader's final arguments were scheduled after Nash's, and they were curious. She did not address the evidence presented during the trial in any great depth, preferring to instead focus on Buono's character. She referred to his "core of humanity" and made peculiar efforts to present his perversions within a framework of moral relativism. She noted that BDSM was currently popular in Los Angeles and that lots of famous individuals such as Lewis Carroll and Ernest Hemingway were sexually attracted to young girls. Did that make them murderers? No. And in ancient Greece, she pointed out, anal sex was just the way it was done.

These arguments, Mader should probably have realized, would not resonate with this jury. They were ordinary people whose concerns were putting food on the table and contributing to the community, not the sexual proclivities of today's youth or dead writers.

Judge George, over defense objections, announced that he would be sequestering the jury until they reached a verdict. These measures were taken to foreclose any accusations of jury tampering, which could easily provoke a mistrial—an unthinkable development after such a lengthy and expensive proceeding. He additionally requested that the jury return a verdict on any single count as soon as they reached agreement.

On 21 October 1983, the jurors were checked into two hotels located close by the criminal courts complex. Until they reached verdicts on all ten counts, they would spend their time there, or in the jury rooms, accompanied twenty-four hours a day by the court bailiffs.

Nobody—not Boren or Nash, nor Salerno or Grogan—was expecting the jury to reach a decision even on any individual count within a day. But all were hopeful that a verdict could be returned on at least one of the strongest counts within the week. They believed that the fiber evidence in the Miller and Wagner cases supported a straightforward guilty verdict.

Their hopes did not materialize. Days passed, and then a week. The jurors then began requesting to see specific trial exhibits again and to receive copies of portions of the testimony to read over.

What did that mean? Surely the decision on those two counts should not require them to review the fine details again? Were they on some other track? Had they missed the point entirely?

Nash and Boren and the detectives worried, waited and speculated. And speculated some more. In the end that's all they could do.

Chapter 36

On 31 October 1983, nine days after deliberations had begun, whatever dead-lock or questions had been tying up the jury finally broke. They announced that they had returned their first verdict.

As predicted, they had made their first decision on the strongest count. Judge George's face was unreadable as he silently absorbed the contents of the small slip of paper and then passed it to the court clerk to be read aloud.

"We, the jury in the above entitled action, find the defendant Angelo Buono guilty of the murder of Lauren Wagner in violation of Section 187, Penal Code, a felony, as charged in Count Eight of the Information and we further find it to be murder in the first degree."

The Wagner case had been Detective Grogan's charge. He wasted little time abandoning the courtroom so he could call Joe Wagner and give him the news.

From there, another delay. Then, on 9 November, the jury returned a verdict of not guilty on the Yolanda Washington count.

Boren and Nash were disappointed, but not surprised. The evidence of Buono's involvement on this count was by far the weakest. The exclusion of LaMieux's testimony had meant the jury essentially only had Bianchi's ac-count of the event to base their decision on. They could not be faulted: they had done their job, in a legal sense.

On 7 November, the jury returned guilty verdicts for the murders of Delores Cepeda, Sonja Johnson and Kimberly Martin. Then a couple days later, guilty verdicts for Kristina Weckler, Lissa Kastin and Jane King.

The final verdict, for Cindy Hudspeth, was not returned until Monday 14 November. The jury had struggled the most in reaching a decision on this count, despite the fact that this murder had the most clear-cut evidence in favor of it being carried out by two men. The killers had pushed Cindy's Datsun over the cliffs of Angeles Crest with her body inside; it therefore seemed obvious that there had to be a second man to drive them away in the other vehicle. Janice Ackers had provided a statement that she had seen two vehicles on the highway at Angeles Crest within the right timeframe. She had not been able to identify Buono; the man she had seen was possibly Bianchi. One of the jurors got stuck on the idea that the killer could have got back down the mountains on a bicycle stashed in the trunk of the Datsun, or that he had taken a bus. As persnickety as this issue sounds, it kept the jury in deadlock for the better part of a week.

In the end they concluded a bicycle was improbable; there had been two killers, and those killers were Bianchi and Buono.

This was, actually, their final reasoning on all the counts, except Washington. Two men. Two killers. Two men seen in key times and locations by several witnesses: Kenneth Bianchi and Angelo Buono.

* * *

After a trial that had dragged on for what seemed an eternity, the penalty phase was blessedly brief, although its outcome was not to everyone's liking.

It was preceded by Angelo Buono's announcement that he was firing his defense team, and was no longer on speaking terms with Gerald Chaleff. Angelo would be representing himself during the penalty stage of the proceeding.

Judge George made every effort to dissuade Buono from this course of action, likening it to asking for the state's help in committing suicide. This, after all, was a capital case in which it was open to the jury to find in favor of the death penalty.

Angelo refused, and on 16 November made his only appearance on the stand.

—My morals and constitutional rights is broken. I ain't taking any procedure in this trial.

Judge George asked Buono to clarify his meaning.

—I stand mute. I stand mute before the law.

His statement was brief and inarticulate, but its message was clear. He might not understand what was going on in the courtroom, but he was innocent, by God, and his ass had been railroaded by the system, man. Taken side by side with the overwhelming evidence of his guilt, it was code for "fuck you".

In the end, the jury made the decision to spare Angelo's life. Buono was sentenced to life imprisonment without the possibility of parole. Judge George did not like the jury's decision; he merely upheld it as was his judicial responsibility. He stated:

"I would not have the slightest reluctance to impose the death penalty in this case were it within my power to do so ... ironically, although these two defendants utilized almost every form of legalized execution against their victims, the defendants have escaped any form of capital punishment."

Nash, Boren, Salerno, Grogan and all who had fought for so many years to see justice done, who had seen first-hand the violated and tortured bodies of the women Buono had killed, were not gratified by the decision either. Nonetheless, they could see the logic in it. All the evidence indicated that Bianchi and Buono had participated equally in the crimes. They had therefore apportioned Buono's punishment as equal to Bianchi's. Ultimately, it was the decision of a fair-minded jury.

Angelo was sent to Calipatria State Prison to serve out his sentence. As for Kenneth Bianchi, Judge George was satisfied, on the basis of his performance on the stand, that he had not met the terms of his plea agreement. He was sent back to Washington, to Walla Walla State Penitentiary.

The cause of the jury's delays in returning verdicts was ultimately revealed to be a schism in the jury room between two camps that had ranged themselves around two men in the group. The jurors had elected Edward McKay as their foreman. The other man didn't like their choice, and with monkey dancing aplenty, what should have been discussions about evidence got bogged down in a turf war. The deadlocks were broken when other jurors switched allegiance.

Then, at the end, Roger Boren and Michael Nash made the troubling discovery that three of the four alternate jurors were opposed to any guilty verdicts at all for Buono. Had any of the principal jurors taken ill during the deliberations, Angelo probably wouldn't have been convicted at all.

The sweet victory represented by the outcome of the trial, Bianchi and Buono's continued existence on the planet notwithstanding, should not obscure the fact that nothing about it was guaranteed. In fact, it had been an incredibly delicate and precarious win for all who had fought so hard. Things could have turned out so very differently. On multiple occasions the trial itself stood teetering on the cliff's edge of abandonment.

Looking back nearly twenty years later, Judge Ronald George said, with a slight air of incredulousness, that what had been most extraordinary to him about the trial was that justice had, in the end, somehow prevailed.

"Against all odds, our legal system ran its course—and worked, as it was intended to."

Postscript

Despite being the most dangerous of killers and rapists, neither Kenneth Bianchi nor Angelo Buono suffered from any lack of romantic opportunities after their imprisonment. In 1986, Buono married Christine Kizuka, the wife of a fellow inmate and a mother of three children who left her husband to be with him. In 1989, Bianchi married Shirlee Book, a pen pal and former love interest of serial killer Ted Bundy. Ken was denied conjugal rights during visits from Shirlee due to his convictions for rape and murder. Both men received thousands of love letters from women all over America and the world.

Angelo Buono died of a heart attack in his cell in 2002. In 2007, his grandson, Christopher Buono, made headlines when he shot his grandmother, Mary Castillo—Angelo's second wife—before turning the gun on himself.

Kenneth Bianchi lives to this day and at sixty-seven is in peak physical condition after years of working out. In prison he gained a law degree and has proved extremely litigious, challenging a company who featured his face in a deck of serial killer playing cards.

Despite IQ testing showing he was only bright-normal in 1979, he has recently tested at 131. Kelli Boyd and her son Ryan still live in the Bellingham area; Ken has no contact with either of them.

The results of analysis of the wrist print lifted from Michelle Maenza's neck were inconclusive. The Alphabet Murders remain unsolved. Bianchi is still a suspect, although he has repeatedly denied any involvement.

Questions about Kenneth Bianchi's mental diagnoses continue despite Judge George's ruling that he faked MPD to escape punishment in the murders of Karen Mandic and Diane Wilder. In 2012 Bianchi struck up a correspondence with author and former British intelligence agent CJ Hart. She reported that

Ken had authored a series of horror novels in the vein of HP Lovecraft that might have been dictated to him by an alter personality. John Watkins has recently stated that he still believes Kenneth Bianchi suffers multiple personality syndrome.

In September 2016 I received a copy of a letter from a true crime enthusiast named Paul Sutherland, who had been corresponding with Bianchi in prison. The letter, penned by Bianchi himself, is the work of a highly intelligent individual of considerable writing ability; he also seems to be either completely delusional or somehow blameless after all—but that, as we have seen, is impossible. His psychopathy is of the shocking degree that he simply does not acknowledge the possibility that he is anything other than a moral and sensitive man who has been destroyed by the criminal justice system. Bianchi insists in the letter that he is innocent of all crimes of which he has been accused, and that the psychiatrists in Washington programmed him with false confessions and memories. He also points to planting of evidence by various police officers involved in the case, including Robert Knudsen.

Bianchi says he likes to watch old Hollywood movies for their innocent outlook and old school morality, "films where something is left to the imagination—or where entertainment does not have to involve mayhem". He dislikes heavy metal and rap music, which to him sounds like "musical instruments being tossed down several flights of stairs".

MPD was removed from the DSM-IV manual and is no longer considered a legitimate psychiatric diagnosis. It was replaced by DID (Dissociative Identity Disorder).

Psychiatry and the criminal justice system continue to struggle with the question of psychopathy, differential diagnosis and mens rea. Defendants on charges of domestic abuse, sexual assault and murder frequently attempt to escape or mitigate punishment on grounds of mental illness. At the same time, community awareness of psychopathy and its relationship to so-called "toxic masculinity" and violence against women is growing.

Following on from incidents of mass violence such as the Orlando Florida shooting, questions are being asked about the light sentences routinely delivered for rape and assault, when increasingly it is understood that men who are dangerous in "small" ways are often dangerous in big ways too.

* * *

Veronica Compton was released from prison on parole in 2003. During her incarceration she became an advocate for prison reform and authored a book about penal rehabilitation called *Eating the Ashes*. She married a political science professor named James Wallace and the two have a daughter. They live in the Seattle area.

Daryl F. Gates, who headed the Hillside Strangler taskforce, remained Chief of the Los Angeles Police Department until 1992. His department tarnished by accusations of extreme brutality and racism, he retired in the wake of the Rodney King beating and ensuing riots.

John Van De Kamp became Attorney General in 1982, taking office from George Deukmejian, with the ironic result that his office presided over the conviction of Buono in a case his office had abandoned two years earlier. His endorsement of Prosecutor Roger Kelly's motion to dismiss the charges against Buono haunted him in his 1990 race for the Democratic nomination for Governor, during which he was "barbecued" over his poor handling of the Hillside Strangler case. He lost the Democratic primary election to Dianne Feinstein.

Roger Boren and Michael Nash went on to illustrious legal careers. Boren was appointed Judge of the Los Angeles Superior Court by George Deukmejian in 1985 and the Court of Appeal in 1987. Nash was appointed to the Los Angeles Municipal Court in 1985 and was elevated to the Superior Court in 1989.

Gerald Chaleff continued his career as a criminal defense attorney and later served on the Webster Commission, which examined the LAPD response to the 1992 civil unrest. In 1997 he became President of the Los Angeles Police Commission. Katherine Mader, after years working in the public defender system, was appointed the LAPD's first Inspector General and became a Deputy Los Angeles County District Attorney in 1999. Today she is a crime author.

Frank Salerno went on to work on several high-profile murder cases including Richard Ramirez, the "Night Stalker". He became a member of the National Planning Committee that created VICAP (Violent Criminal Apprehension Program) which pioneered federal coordination in the hunt for serial murderers. Bob Grogan continued to work in homicide for the LAPD for several years. He left Los Angeles for Sedona in the early nineties and returned to his first love, music, playing keyboards for several jazz groups.

Judge Ronald George became Associate Justice of the Supreme Court of California in 1991 and the Chief Justice of California in 1996. In 2008, he authored the Supreme Court's ruling legalizing same-sex marriage in California. He retired in 2011.

Lois Lee received her PhD in 1981. She founded Children of the Night, a major non-profit supporting youth involved in sex trafficking. Her research is now an official reference for police and the criminal justice system in the treatment of child prostitutes. Since 1988 she has served as an expert witness for federal and state prosecutors enforcing laws against dangerous pimps, and has received several humanitarian awards.

In the mid-2010s, significant tactical changes were finally made in the war on prostitution in Los Angeles, with greater efforts aimed towards arrest and prosecution of johns and pimps, and the introduction of counselling and redirection programs for sex workers. The other side of the story is that LA prostitutes are getting younger and younger. Pimps now routinely groom kids as young as thirteen into the sex industry.

The commercial sex industry in all its forms has never been more visible or pervasive. To place the heinous crimes of Bianchi and Buono in context, we should not overlook that whatever else was wrong with these very sick men, they were also guys who, like many others, were raised on a steady diet of pornography and prostitution, and suffered an overweening sense of sexual entitlement. Their actions must be situated in the social field from which they sadly, in significant measure, arose: the world in which women have historically been denied ownership over their bodies, and have had their individual identities subsumed to the exploitation of those bodies.

From the vantage point of the present, the full realities of this case laid out herewith are truly a lesson in the banality of evil. The sobering story of this case's passage through the courts similarly contains strong warnings for the treatment of sex crime within the contemporary criminal justice sphere. The garish formal narrative of this case which has dominated to the present time, emphasizing Bianchi and Buono's place in the serial killer canon, should never disguise from us the fact that two men raped and murdered ten women—and nearly got away with it, with the sanction of the highest offices of justice.

Dear reader,

We hope you enjoyed reading *Killing Cousins*. Please take a moment to leave a review in Amazon, even if it's a short one. Your opinion is important to us.

Discover more books by O.J. Modjeska at
https://www.nextchapter.pub/authors/oj-modjeska

Want to know when one of our books is free or discounted for Kindle? Join the newsletter at http://eepurl.com/bqqB3H

Best regards,

O.J. Modjeska and the Next Chapter Team

Books by OJ Modjeska

Did you enjoy *Murder by Increments*? Remember to subscribe to OJ's mailing list at the link below to receive notifications of new releases. And don't forget to grab a copy of OJ's aviation disaster ebook bestseller, *Gone: Catastrophe in Paradise*, available now.

http://ojmodjeska.blogspot.com.au

www.estoire.co

Books published by Next Chapter

Gone - Catastrophe In Paradise
A City Owned (Murder by Increments Book 1)
Killing Cousins (Murder by Increments Book 2)

You might also like:

Prisoner 4374 by A.J. Griffiths-Jones

To read first chapter for free, head to:
https://www.nextchapter.pub/books/prisoner-4374